Island on the Edge of the World

Charles Maclean

Island on the Edge of the World
the story of St Kilda

'...the isle of Irte, which is agreed to be
under the Circius and on the margine of the
world, beyond which there is found no land
in these bounds.'

John of Fordun

CANONGATE · Edinburgh

First published in 1972 by Tom Stacey Ltd
Revised edition published in 1977
by Canongate Publishing Limited
17 Jeffrey Street, Edinburgh
Paperback edition published in 1983
Reprinted in 1987

ISBN 0 86241 045 2

Printed and bound in Great Britain
by Billing and Sons Ltd, Worcester

Acknowledgements

My thanks are due to the National Trust for Scotland, whose help
and co-operation in so many areas of research has been invaluable, to
the Nature Conservancy, the Ministry of Defence and the School of
Scottish Studies. I would also like to thank Catherine Armet, Robert
Atkinson, the Marquis of Bute, the Dowager Marchioness of Bute,
Donald Erskine, Crispin Fisher, Neil Gillies, Eric Hosking, Basil
Megaw, Ralph Morton, Jock Nimlin, Lady Jean Rankin, Tom Scott
and Donald Stewart. In particular I am indebted to Edward Gold-
smith for his inspiration and encouragement.

for Valerie

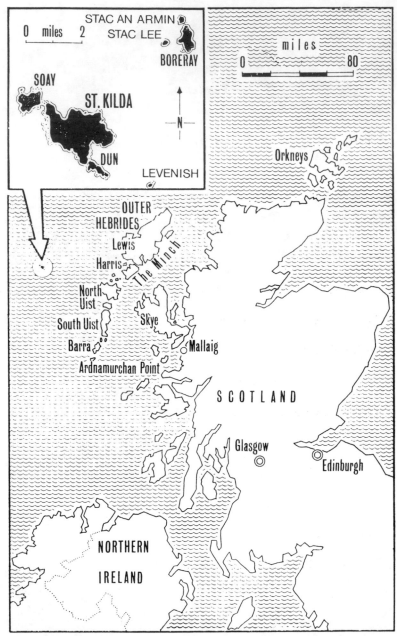

St Kilda in relation to Scotland and the Hebrides

Contents

List of Illustrations

Between pages 16 and 17

St Kildans with telescope *National Trust for Scotland*
St Kilda from the north-east *Eric J. Hosking*
Village Bay *Eric J. Hosking*
Stac Lee from the east *Robert Atkinson*
Cliff walking on Oiseval *National Trust for Scotland*
The Isle of Soay *Eric J. Hosking*
Euphemia MacCrimmon, the poetess *School of Scottish Studies*
Married women *c.* 1890 *National Trust for Scotland*
Fowlers relaxing at the cliff's edge *National Trust for Scotland*
Selling souvenirs to tourists *George Outram & Co.*
Finlay MacQueen, his son and grandson in 1927 *National Trust for Scotland*
A St Kilda fowler *Niall Rankin*
Finlay MacQueen talking to John Mackenzie *National Trust for Scotland*
St Kilda knitwear: gloves, socks and scarves
Cill-Chriosed, the graveyard on Hirta
Interior of the church *Robert Atkinson*
Old woman with child *National Trust for Scotland*
Bird fowling on cliffs
Rev. John Mackay *School of Scottish Studies*
Church and manse *George Outram & Co.*
The St Kilda parliament *National Trust for Scotland*
Woman knitting *National Trust for Scotland*
Man with sack of wool *National Trust for Scotland*

Between pages 96 and 97

St Kildan schoolchildren *Edinburgh Public Libraries*
Two St Kildan children *National Trust for Scotland*
Sending a letter by St Kilda 'mailboat' *Robert Atkinson*
Dividing the fulmar catch *c.* 1890 *National Trust for Scotland*
Finlay MacQueen with his daughter and younger brother *c.* 1904
An artist's impression of fowling in 1891 *A. Jobling*
Rachel Anne Gillies *National Trust for Scotland*
Neil Ferguson and Donald MacQueen grinding corn in a quern *National Trust for Scotland*

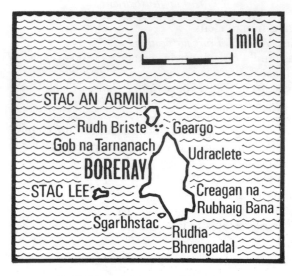

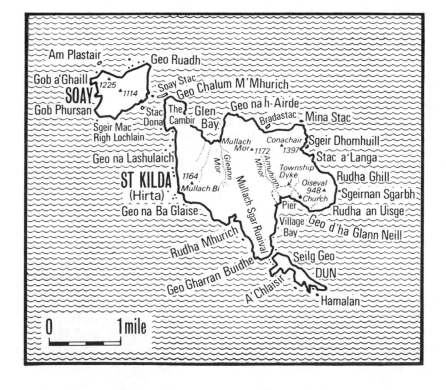

St Kilda and its satellite islands

Introduction

When a simple or primitive society comes into contact with civilization it undergoes cultural change. Unable to resist the seductive advantages of a more developed technology, it also embraces or has forced upon it a new system of values which inevitably leads to the breakdown of the old culture. This process of acculturation can be seen today as instrumental not only in the destruction of large numbers of simple societies in underdeveloped parts of the world, but also as a cause of social and environmental problems in the increasingly homogeneous wasteland of modern civilization. It is illustrated here in microcosm by the story of the remote Hebridean island of St Kilda.

A part of Britain but a world apart, St Kilda society existed in almost complete isolation from the mainstream of civilization for more than a thousand years. Increased contact with the mainland during the 19th century brought about the slow downfall of what many had once regarded as an ideal society. In 1930 the islanders who could no longer support themselves, were finally evacuated at their own request.

The history of St Kilda exists by virtue of those visitors, who by going to the island helped to give it a history in the first place and by writing about it afterwards recorded what would otherwise have been lost. Since the St Kildans themselves were mostly illiterate until the turn of the century, their story is chiefly told by outsiders, who, however unwittingly, contributed to the destruction of the island society by breaking its isolation. But without them there would have been no story to tell.

The man whose pen first made St Kilda famous was undoubtedly Martin Martin, the gentleman from the Isle of Skye, hired as literary tutor to the MacLeods of Dunvegan. Martin, who travelled extensively among the Western Isles of Scotland and wrote about most of them, visited St Kilda in 1697. His account of the islanders and their way of life in *A Late Voyage to St Kilda* is a brilliant and individual piece of rapportage displaying keen powers of observation and, in spite of Dr Johnson's assertions to the contrary, a distinct literary gift. Martin's work provided the later authors of St Kilda with a source of inspiration, unique information about the island and set a high level of achievement. A few of his successors, like the Rev Kenneth Macaulay, a minister from Ardnamurchan and a great uncle to the famous historian, who was sent to St Kilda in 1758 as a missionary, managed to write close to Martin's standard. Each successive publication about St Kilda (there has been a surprising number) has nonetheless added to the sum total of knowledge on the subject in one way or another and will no doubt continue to do so. In the present book I have drawn information and quoted liberally from many of St Kilda's authors especially Martin and Macaulay, to whom I am widely indebted.

After the evacuation of St Kilda the owner, Sir Reginald MacLeod, sold the island in 1932 to the Marquis of Bute, who as an eminent ornithologist was particularly interested in preserving it as a bird sanctuary and bequeathed it on his death to the National Trust for Scotland. The island has since been made a nature reserve and is leased by the Trust to the Nature Conservancy, who are making an ecological survey of the wildlife, noting any changes that have occurred since the departure of the islanders. During the summer months the National Trust runs cruises to St Kilda and organizes parties to go out and spend a fortnight or so living in three restored cottages on the island and work at the repair and restoration of the buildings, cottages, cleits, dykes and other remains of St Kildan civilization. Eventually they hope to reclaim the entire village from what would otherwise be certain devastation by wind and weather. In 1957 a small area on Hirta was commandeered by the Ministry of Defence for a missile tracking station. A few years ago £500,000 was spent on lengthening the pier in Village Bay and erecting new buildings for a military camp, which surprisingly has been quite well landscaped. It is ironical nonetheless that so much money and effort should have been made available for this purpose forty years after the islanders were evacuated.

Finding the archipelago of St Kilda on the map is not always easy. A map of Scotland which includes the Outer Hebrides, will often leave out St Kilda because it cannot be fitted on to the page and is too small to qualify for an inset of its own. The island group, comprising four islands—Hirta, Soay, Boreray and Dun (Hirta, also known as St Kilda, is much the largest)—lies out in the Atlantic Ocean on the edge of the continental shelf, about fifty miles due west of Harris and 110 miles west of the nearest land on the mainland. Its isolation is increased by the difficulties of getting there. Until the 19th century the voyage involved several days and nights in an open boat rowed by MacLeod's men from Skye. Once beyond the relative safety of the Minch they were at the mercy of the open Atlantic. If the weather turned bad retreat if possible to the shelter of the Outer Hebrides was the only hope. Even today a boat setting out for St Kilda is by no means assured of reaching its destination.

The islands are almost entirely cliff-girt and surrounded by deep water. The only point where it is possible to make a safe landing or lie at anchor is in Village Bay. When a strong wind blows from the south-east straight into the Bay this one place of refuge becomes untenable. A large boat can usually lie off and ride out a storm but an ordinary fishing vessel may be forced to return to North Uist or Harris and wait for the wind to change or die down before making another attempt. Until the turn of the century when conditions were right for anchoring in the Bay a landing could only be made in a small dinghy since it was impossible to bring a larger boat into the rocks. Although a concrete pier was built in 1902 and has been enlarged and improved more recently, the situation has hardly changed and most landings and embarkations still have to be made by small boat, unless one travels by army landing craft, which pulls up on the beach and disgorges its cargo from gaping bows directly on to dry land. This peculiarly sick-making form of transport, which is perhaps the easiest way of getting to St Kilda, rolls like a pig in heavy seas and takes nearly twelve hours to do the trip from the Outer Hebrides.

Without owning or chartering a boat, the only other way of seeing the island is on a National Trust cruise or as a member of one of the Trust working parties. None of these alternatives, however, can guarantee dates of arrival and departure, nor with the exception of private transport do they offer much choice in the length of one's visit. The Army landing craft stays for only six hours on the island, goes out with the tide and returns again a fortnight later. The Trust cruises and working parties represent two similar extremes. St Kilda is still a difficult place to get to and from and for this very reason retains its identity despite the encroachments of the Ministry of Defence. The remoteness of the island and the power of the surrounding ocean, which together played such a crucial role in the history of the island when it was inhabited, have relinquished none of their former control.

CHARLES MACLEAN 1972

CHAPTER ONE

The Island

'Away with systems! Away with a corrupt world!
Let us breathe the air of the Enchanted island.'

GEORGE MEREDITH

A dark extravagant shape slowly detached itself from the grey overall of sea and sky. As we made a path towards it, following convergent streams of sea-birds across the rolling hills of the Atlantic, it turned under a watery sun the whitish green of Pernod and proclaimed itself an island. The colour improved the closer we sailed; the outline sharpened; a second land-mass moved out from behind the first. Shoulders of cliffs descended into the ocean and re-emerged as stacs and skerries, standing up out of the water like elbows and knees at angles of defiance. A ragged promontory extended a treacherous arm, as we passed between it and a pyramid of rock, which stood by itself pale and massive in the middle of that forbidding sea-waste and guarded the entrance to St Kilda.

On rounding the point of the promontory our boat came out of the Atlantic swell and entered the disconcertingly calm waters of a horseshoe bay surrounded on three sides by green amphitheatrical hills. As we approached the beach at the far end of the bay individual features of the landscape began to define themselves more clearly and the general impression of strangeness gave place to one more particular. From afar the green effect of the island had camouflaged the variety of its component colours, which were now revealed in patches of brilliant and dullest green, of dark to pale brown, and violet, and in the whites, greys, yellows and blacks of stone, loose scree and bald faces of rock. In that curious westerly light, drawn from the reflective expanses of sea and sky, the colours of St Kilda seemed to permeate the atmosphere with the rhythms of soft luminous energy. It gave to the island a magical quality which seemed familiar because half-remembered from dreams.

Upon the first sight and sensation of Hirta, signs of human habitation follow as a disappointment. Buildings scarcely impinge on the landscape. The army camp in a corner of the bay close to the sea is too obviously transient and its purpose too foreign to the island to be of consequence. The ruined cottages of the village, the stone dykes which divide the sloping land, the stone pens which once folded the islanders' sheep, the innumerable stone cleits where they stored their food—these, the last remains of the old community seem equally small and insignificant. They merge too well with their background, and as time and the winds take their toll, gradually become more and more difficult to distinguish from the random heaps of grey stone which litter the hillsides. It is as if the human influence which once kept them apart has been lacking for too long.

Ashore things take on a different aspect. Along the grassy village street the roofless cottages, overgrown with weeds and cluttered with piles of fallen masonry, still give an intimation of the perpetuity that once belonged here. Behind the village the dykes and pens still standing, apart from a fall of stone here and there, recall their former purpose as the dark Soay sheep now wander nonchalantly among them and in and out of the empty houses. Three of the cottages have been restored, their roofs replaced, windows and doors put back; smoke trickles from their chimneys completing a picture of what they must have looked like some forty years ago. The whole village with its long curving line of empty shells is for a moment eloquent of its desertion, but it is these slight signs of life, the frail but heartening scent of a peat fire, the pitch roof glistening and melting a little in the rays of the sun, that evoke the ineffable sadness of evacuation.

The view of Hirta from Village Bay gives a false impression of the island; the serenity of the landscape is misleading, its gentle contours deceptive. But climb the slopes of Conachair and from the top catch first sight of the cliffs as they fall away sheer more than a thousand feet to the Atlantic below and one suddenly realizes that these rounded hills have no backs to them. In façade they sweep up to their summits then stop, as though bitten through the middle. The cliffs of Conachair come upon one as unexpectedly as news of a death. After the first awful moment one can do little more than lie down and take a deep breath, then perhaps slowly crawl forwards still in a horizontal position, which is only a little better than standing, and peer over the edge.

The ocean below looks the way it does from an aeroplane, without movement, unreal. Only the fulmar like miniature albatrosses, gliding about in apparently aimless but beautiful flight, give any

(a) St Kildans with telescope

(b) **St Kilda** from the north-east showing the Gap between Oiseval and Conachair. The island's rounded hills have no backs to them. In places they fall sheer from more than 1,000 feet to the Atlantic below.

(a) Cliff-walking on Oiseval with Stac Levenish visible seawards.

(b) Stac Lee from the east whitened by gannets and their guano.

(c) The Isle of Soay, the second largest landmass in the archipelago to the NW of the main island, takes the full brunt of wind and ocean.

(d) Village Bay flanked by the rocky islet of Dun, offers St Kilda's only landing place and anchorage.

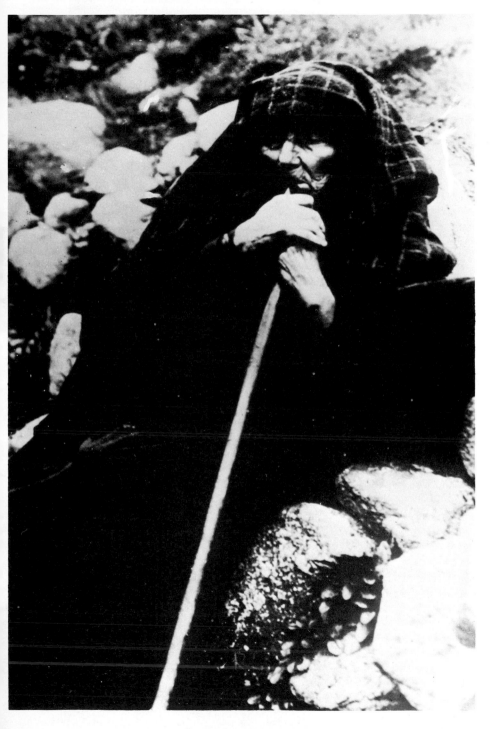

Euphemia MacCrimmon, the poetess, aged about 84. It is to her and Alexander Carmichael that we owe the few surviving examples of St Kilda poetry and song.

c

g

(a) Married women *c.* 1890 were distinguished by white frill in the front of their headdresses.

(b) Fowlers relaxing at the cliff's edge with Boreray in the background.

(c) Selling souvenirs to tourists was latterly an important source of income to the islanders

(d) Finlay MacQueen, his son and grandson in 1927

(e) A St Kilda fowler with his catch of fulmar
(f) Finlay MacQueen talking to the factor John Mackenzie

(g) Gloves, socks and scarves were knitted by the women both for export and the tourist trade

(a) Old woman with child

(b) Cill-Chriosed, the graveyard on Hirta bears witness to the departed community's lonely struggle for existence

(c) Bird Fowling on cliffs

(d) The Rev John Mackay, minister on St Kilda from 1865–89, established a harsh sabbatarian rule over his parishioners

(e) The interior of the church, damp, bleak and dominated by the pulpit

(f) The church and manse (nearest to the sea), where the islanders often spent up to nine or ten hours on Sunday, were built in 1830

e

(a) The St Kilda Parliament, composed of all the grown men on the island, met every morning except Sunday in the Street. Its most important function was to decide what work should be done that day.

(b) Woman knitting.

(c) Man with sack of wool.

idea of perspective. They fly close to one's head landing on nearby ledges; fat and friendly birds, their short bodies and bull necks seem to disappear into their broad elegant wingspans. As they descend the cliff-face the eye in fright follows them down, jealous of their extraordinary gliding skill, until they become tiny white specks hovering and swirling at random far below. One gets the impression not so much of looking down at the sea, but up at a night sky full of stars or snow flakes. A sense of scale is unavailable for want of a boat or some other familiar object in the sea below. But sometimes a diving gannet observed from above can realize the vast size of the cliffs. Seen from a height of 1,000 feet the gannet, perhaps 900 feet below (its brilliant white colouring making it easy to recognize), dives the remaining 100 feet into the sea. It is no bigger than a crumb of glass when it begins its dive, but the time it takes to hit the water and disappear from sight is long enough to fill the coolest head with vertigo.

The cacophony of voices, which forms an unending barrier of sound along the cliff's edge, is almost as unnerving as the absurdities of scale. The sea-birds all have their different cries, some of them wild and hideous, others more comfortingly human. At times the singing of grey seals can be heard faint and drifting like the music of sirens. But eeriest is the wind, which sighs and moans through the caves at sea level and throws up its complaints to the cliff tops strangely distorted, inviting one down.

Returning from the margin to the relative safety of the top of Conachair, the whole panorama of the archipelago is clearly visible. It is one of the great attractions of a small island if one can see all its limits from its highest point. On most days St Kilda has a round and empty horizon, but in fine weather, when the cloud lifts and visibility is good, a narrow blue line of land appears low in the east and the long chain of the Outer Hebrides can be made out with the naked eye. It does little, however, to moderate the feeling of primordial isolation which this view of the world inspires. It is a feeling compounded by an overwhelming sense of human frailty as one is forced to bear constant witness to the most basic processes of nature, as the land beneath one's feet, lying in defiance of the ocean and the winds, fights a slow, elemental and losing battle against them.

Hirta was once part of a much larger land-mass and joined to the other small islands in the group, but over the millennia, erosion caused by direct exposure to the Atlantic has worked spectacular changes. Where once there must have been gentle slopes running down to the sea, there are now massive cliffs on all sides except for a small area covered by the two bays.

The island is made up of igneous rocks formed by volcanic action in the tertiary geological period. They can be roughly divided into light coloured granite on the eastern side of Hirta and much darker gabbro, which is found more to the west where the cliffs are craggiest. All around the coast the effect of wind and waves can be seen in the fantastic shapes and compilations of rock, in the gaping caves and gigantic flying buttresses, in the towering stacs and broken down skerries, which compass the island. The relentlessness of these powers of destruction at times becomes almost unbearable.

Nowhere is their influence more evident than on the long ragged island of Dun, which shields Village Bay from the Atlantic and is separated from Hirta by a narrow gut, known as the Gap, little more than fifty yards wide. The Dun is a rocky precipitous ridge a mile long and varying in width between 100 and 200 feet. On its south-western coast the tempestuous climate has torn and split the rock without mercy, but on the Bay side its steep slopes are covered with lush green vegetation. At one point the Dun is pierced by a high natural tunnel, through which the sea flows, and where in time yet another island will be formed when the arch gives way.

Such is the pattern of erosion. Once a promontory has been created, the sea makes a tunnel through it and widens the gap until the roof collapses leaving an island or less, a stac, which eventually is worn down to a skerry and finally submerged. This inexorable process usually takes thousands of years to complete, but in one case on Hirta it was speeded up by the intervention of man. Mina Stac is a high rock at the foot of the cliffs of Conachair now separated from the main island by a deep channel. In the 16th century it was still connected to Hirta by a narrow archway, but after the dispersal of the Spanish Armada, one of the galleons lost in St Kilda waters was driven through the channel in a storm. The ship's mast caught the arch as it passed underneath it and brought a massive fall of rock down on to its decks, sinking the ship and destroying the arch.

To the north side of Hirta, to the wild end of the island, separated from the village glen by a high ridge, lies Glen Bay. It has no beach but it is possible to climb down to where the rock shelves modestly into the sea, though the prospect is hardly inviting. This part of the island has not been inhabited for more than a thousand years and still holds on to the darkness of its primitive past. The bizarre stone shapes silhouetted along the horizon from Mullach Bi to the Cambir, the bareness of the turf swept by Atlantic gales, the prehistoric structures and crumbling cleits in Gleann Mor, and the steep oppressive walls of the glen, all help 'o sever its connection with linear time. Scattered pieces of aeroplane wreckage, of twisted aluminium whitened by rain like gnarled bones, still lying where they fell out on the hillside, do nothing to dispel the atmosphere of ancient gloom.

Just as Village Bay is flanked by the island of Dun, so is Glen Bay protected from the full fury of the west wind by Soay. Cut off from Hirta by a narrow stac-filled strait the Isle of Soay lies opposite the Cambir to the north-west of the main island. It is the second largest land-mass in the archipelago and entirely cliff-girt, but grassy on its flattish top with sea-thrift and purple vetch growing on the ledges to its sheltered side. Near to the highest point on the island, some 1,200 feet above sea-level, there is a collection of stones, which the St Kildans used to call 'the altar', though its significance has long been forgotten.

Equally cliff-bound and even more impressive than Soay, Boreray lies four miles to the north-east of Hirta, though the distance seems much shorter. The west side of the island presents a sheer face of cliff to the Atlantic rising in places to over 1,000 feet. But much of its splendour Boreray owes to its attendant stacs, Armin to the north (at 627 feet the highest sea-rock in the British Isles), and Lee to the south-west. White-washed with the guano of countless thousands of gannets, they rise out of the sea like the sternest most implacable monsters of the imagination.

It is likely that at one time Boreray was inhabited by man, but in recent history the St Kildans used only to visit the island on fowling expeditions or to tend the sheep pastured there. Sometimes the men would stay for a week or more, living in the old underground houses and communicating if necessary with the main island by turning up patches of turf on the hillside facing Hirta. They had three signals. If they turned up turf to the left of a certain spot it meant that the party was running short of food and water and needed a boat to come over with provisions. A patch revealed to the right meant that one of the party had been injured or taken ill. A very large patch signified a death.

Any such expedition by boat to one of the other islands was dependent on the clemency of the weather. In St Kilda the climate played a decisive part in the lives of the inhabitants and on the whole added to their isolation. The frequent storms which blow from September to April often made it impossible to get on or off the island for weeks if not months at a time. Even in summer the weather can be very changeable. A sunny day with blue sky and a calm sea will turn into a raging gale in a matter of hours and with little warning for anyone out in a boat.

The wind blows with terrific force, sometimes gusting up to 130 mph or more, flattening the tops of the giant waves and sending sheets of spray two or three hundred feet up into the air over the top of the Dun. It strips bare the hillside, tearing up turf wherever it can catch hold, killing heather and grass by exposing their roots. After a rainstorm the whole island is left awash. The water runs straight off the hills and, in the days of the St Kildans, could do serious damage to crops, especially when combined with high winds and salt spray. Sometimes it rains for two or three weeks without stopping, but on average the rainfall is much the same as that of the Outer Hebrides—about fifty inches, most of which falls in the mid-winter months of December and January. In winter the days are very short—just as at midsummer the night is only an hour long—but apart from bouts of frost and sometimes a fall of snow, which never lies for long, the climate stays mild. In summer there are occasionally long spells of clear, warm weather, when, because of its shape, the island becomes a sun-trap and almost too hot. But more often the hills are swathed in 'ambient white mists', as Martin Martin called them, for, being so high St Kilda makes its own cloud. When approaching or leaving the group in fine weather the cloud cap above Conachair and Oiseval is usually the first and last sight to be had of the islands.

Perhaps the most interesting feature which once concerned the climate, now more the geology of St Kilda, is that there is no evidence to suggest that the islands were covered by the continental ice-sheet in the quaternary period of glaciation. And during the last Ice Age, about 10,000 years ago, which froze over most of Britain, it is thought that the ice barrier ran down between St Kilda and the Outer Hebrides. The islands, therefore, were never completely glaciated, though the sea would have been full of icebergs and the glens and corries of Hirta may have carried light glaciers. The significance of this lies in the strong possibility that some forms of life may have survived from an earlier and much warmer interglacial period.

'There is no sort of trees, no, not the least shrub grows here, nor ever a bee seen at any time,' wrote Martin in 1697. He went on to describe how some St Kildans, who once paid a visit to Skye, were amazed by the trees there and tried to take some back to Hirta, but soon got tired of carrying them, as they were on foot and not used to walking long distances. A later account of St Kilda, however, mentions that the trunks of trees were often found buried in peat deposits. This is supported by recent pollen analysis, which has shown that at one time alder, hazel, birch, Scots pine, elm and oak all grew on the island, even at heights of 1,000 feet and more, where surprisingly the heaviest tree pollen counts were recorded. But for the last 1,500–2,000 years St Kilda has been bare of trees and any attempts to grow them now, with the possible exception of rowan or spruce, would almost certainly meet with failure.

Some time before the last Ice Age, when the climate was milder and the island lightly forested, wrens first migrated to Hirta. As the climate began to deteriorate and the environment to change, the wrens had to adapt to survive. Trees gradually ceased to grow on the island and the wrens had to learn to perch on the rocks and cliffs instead, often in high winds. Consequently they evolved certain adaptive traits. They developed larger and stronger feet, longer tougher beaks and grew generally bigger than the mainland birds. Their colouring became drabber though more varied, and their song peculiarly sweet and soft. They now constitute a highly differentiated sub-species known as *troglodytes hirtensis*—the St Kilda wren.

When it was recognized as a sub-species in 1884 the St Kilda wren was mercilessly hunted by ornithologists, egg-collectors, taxidermists and tourists, until in 1888 it was declared to be in danger of becoming extinct. Unfortunately, in this case, St Kilda had been exempted from the Wild Birds Protection Act of 1880, because of the islanders' dependence on sea-birds and their eggs for food. There was no way of stopping the slaughter. In 1904, however, a special act of parliament was passed to protect the St Kilda wren and Leach's fork-tailed petrel. Gradually the wrens recovered and now there are more than a hundred breeding pairs. They are often to be seen up behind the village in amongst the old cleits and drystone dykes, where they flit over the surface of the stone with a scurrying movement, which is more characteristic of lizards than birds. When they settle, despite their extra size and strength, they seem remarkably small and delicate.

Until a few years after the evacuation St Kilda also possessed two sub-species of mouse—a house mouse (*mus muralis*) and a field mouse (*mus hirtensis*). The field mouse, which was almost certainly on the island before the last Ice Age, has survived to the present day. It weighs twice as much as the mainland species and its ears and hind feet are larger. Its tail is as long as its body and its coat is rust coloured on top and yellowish underneath. The house mouse, which became extinct in 1938, was equally differentiated from its mainland counterpart. Again it was longer, hairier, coloured differently and had a different shaped skull to the ordinary mouse.

When the island was excavated in 1930 the house mouse's source of food and warmth disappeared. Those that survived the large number of cats, which the St Kildans left behind them, were forced to enter into competition with the stronger and expanding population of field mice for shelter and food. The house mice soon died out. Closely related species can never share the same habitat unless they are living in different homes and have different food supplies —each must have its distinct ecological niche. For this reason it seems unlikely that the house mouse could have existed on Hirta before the arrival of its human benefactors.

In 1885 the mouse was described as St Kilda's only wild animal, the lion of the island, in fear of whom went nothing larger than an earwig or a spider. Frogs, toads, lizards, snakes, rats, rabbits and hares were and still are quite unknown in those parts. Since 1932, however, the mouse has had to give up its throne, or a part of it, to the Soay sheep, about a hundred of which were taken from Soay and settled on Hirta. The population, which exists in a wild state, thrived and now numbers more than 1,500.

According to tradition a Viking by the name of Callum brought the first sheep to Soay, but they may well have come at a much earlier date with Neolithic settlers. Soay sheep are a primitive breed descended from the wild moufflon at an early stage in its domestication. Remains of the same breed have been found in prehistoric settlements in the Borders and in Europe, but St Kilda is its last native habitat in Britain. In 1527 Boece first described Soay sheep as 'wild beasts not very different from sheep. The hair is long and tallie (drab) neither like the wool of sheep nor goat.' Although brief the description is fairly accurate. The colour of the sheep ranges from a rich chocolate brown to a light shade of biscuit, though the greater proportion are dark. They have short tails and a soft wool fleece, which comes away in spring leaving them with a shorter hair coat for the summer months. Their long legs, which enable them to run extremely fast, give them the look and agility of mountain goats. From the cliff's edge one can often see them cropping the grass from narrow ledges hundreds of feet below in places that would seem totally inaccessible. Close to—if one can get near to them for they are mostly very shy—they are attractive animals. The black horns of the rams sweep up from the head and curve in towards the shoulders and out again, giving them a fierce but noble bearing. The faces of the ewes and lambs, however, have great charm and reveal, as one might expect, a more intelligent expression than is usual among domesticated breeds of sheep.

The ecology and indeed the whole character of St Kilda is dominated by the three species of sea-birds upon which the islanders once depended for their livelihood. The enormous colonies of gannets, fulmar and puffins not only provide the land with fertilizer but the sea with plankton from their guano. The incessant clamour of their cries fills the air and their myriad flights divide the sky. But unless one has seen the gannets on Stac Lee, the fulmar on the cliffs of Conachair or the puffins on the Dun, bare statistics and even exaggerated descriptions of their numbers are unconvincing. Until a later chapter let it be enough to say that between them these three birds own the archipelago.

One species of sea-bird, which though small in number makes its presence felt on Hirta, is the Great Skua. In summer there are usually several pairs of these large, unsympathetic predators holding territory between the heights of Conachair and Mullach Mhor. To walk here alone along the cliff's edge is not always advisable. The first rush of great brown wings about one's ears and the glimpsed close-ups of angry eyes and a vicious beak is enough to alarm even the most intrepid bird-man. Nor do skuas let up after the first display of aggression, and what may have started out as a pleasant cliff-walk can soon turn into a nightmare routine of falling to the ground trying to cover one's head as the birds sweep out of the sky in repeated attacks. It is an experience not to be forgotten.

Many other less aggressive sea-birds are found in St Kilda including guillemots, razorbills, kittiwakes, Manx shearwaters, storm petrels, Leach's fork-tailed petrels and several species of gull. Land birds too, use Hirta as a resting place during their migration in spring and autumn. In spring, particularly, and early summer the profusion and variety of birdlife on the islands is extraordinary and provides plenty of opportunity for ornithologists. To the St Kildans, however, the birds meant more than a subject for scientific study. They were the most welcome visitors they ever saw. The year after the evacuation one of the islanders wrote in a letter to a friend that it was indeed sad because for the first time in who knows how many years 'there would be no one in Hirta this spring to welcome home the birds'.

The history of the St Kildans is essentially the story of a bird culture, of a people whose existence was dependent upon those sea-birds, which provided them with food, medicine, lighting, manure, shoes, a source of revenue, a way of life and often enough, when they broke their necks trying to catch them, a cause of death. In winter when the birds were gone and left the skies vacant, when the only sounds were of the howling wind driving storm clouds in from the Atlantic and of the great ocean rollers crashing against the Dun, life in St Kilda was hard, a lonely struggle for survival, which, when the islanders came to know of other things, was to seem no longer worth the effort. But for two thousand years they knew little or nothing of the outside world and could make no comparisons with an easier type of existence. Impoverished perhaps by this lack of contact and restricted by the limitations of their circumstances they nonetheless enjoyed a life of peace and contentment which at times could even be idyllic. If they had been less innocent of the world their society would not have been viable. The final breaking of their isolation, the late encounter with civilization, which so few primitive peoples are able to withstand, was to destroy them equally.

CHAPTER TWO

Early History

Roughly ten thousand years ago, when Mesolithic hunter-gatherers still roamed Britain subsisting hardly along the dark forest edges and blown shores of the sea, far away in a low, green tract of land, known as the Fertile Crescent, which reached from the delta of the Tigris and Euphrates to the valley of the lower Nile, small bands of Neolithic people had already begun to till the ground, sow seed and raise the first crops. They tamed the wild sheep, herded goats and pigs and eventually domesticated a breed of long-horned cattle. The animals interacted with the crops, providing manure in return for better pasture, and thus co-operated with man in what are believed to have been the beginnings of agriculture. Neolithic farming and the more permanent village settlements which accompanied this new way of life, soon led to a rapid development in the size and spread of human populations. In search of new pastures they slowly slashed and burned their way north across the European steppes and westwards through the countries of the Mediterranean to the Atlantic coast.

The first Neolithic settlers to reach Britain probably came over from Northern France by the Atlantic route c. 3500 BC and migrated up the west coast, always staying within sight of land, as far as the Shetland Isles. The colder climate of Europe was more conducive to the tending of flocks than to cultivation, but both activities required open unforested land. In Britain the Neolithic settlers, who were sea-people as well as farmers, found that the coastal land cleared of heavy forest by wind and salt spray, best provided for their needs, as it had for the Mesolithic nomads before them. Over the next thousand years or so these two peoples gradually merged to produce an expanding population of indigenous British cultures.

Islands in particular made attractive sites for settlement. As well as offering natural protection against invasion, they were usually only lightly wooded and provided good opportunity for both farming and fishing. In Scotland the earliest Neolithic settlers and

megalith builders seem to have preferred the Orkneys and Shet-
lands to the Western Isles, and in the Hebrides most Neolithic
remains belong to a later period. There is evidence, however, of a
settlement on Harris dating back to 4000 BC, which suggests that
very early pioneering expeditions may have taken place along a
part of the Atlantic route, which was later discontinued.

St Kilda was visible from the Hebrides and must have seemed
particularly suitable for settlement being so green, lush and isolated,
but whether it was first colonized at this early stage or at a much
later date can only be a matter of speculation until a complete
archaeological analysis of the island has been carried out. Unfortunately the study of St Kilda's antiquities has not been made easier
by the islanders' age-old practice of destroying ancient buildings
and using the stones to put up new ones in much the same style
Neolithic underground chambers, Bronze Age cairns and Iron Age
hut circles have all been found on the islands, but as yet little that
is definite is known about any of them.

One of the hypogea on Hirta, which can be seen today, was
opened up by John Sands when he visited the island in 1877. The
Earth House or House of Fairies, as it was known, had been buried
with scant respect beneath a potato patch, which had to be indemnified before the excavation was allowed to begin. Like other underground houses in the Hebrides it consisted of a central chamber,
approached by a tunnel, with a roof of stone slabs flush with the
ground, and stone walls, into which were let several smaller com-
partments for sleeping and storage. Below a two-foot layer of peat
and ashes Sands unearthed a flag-stone floor which drained into one
corner of the central chamber. Buried in the peat he found a
quantity of limpet shells, which had been cooked on a fire, fulmar
and gannet carcases, sheep and cattle bones and various stone implements. The tools were easily recognized by the St Kildans of the
day, who could even put names to them, for the equivalent of many
of them were still in use. The animal remains showed that the diet
of the St Kildans had changed little over the millennia. Although
it makes it easier to imagine what life on the island was like at any
time in the past, the atavistic life-style of the inhabitants adds considerably to the problem of differentiating between the various stages
in their early history.

Like their descendants after them, the earliest settlers in St Kilda
were a pastoral society, who cultivated only a small amount of land.
They herded sheep and cattle, but supplemented their diet with
fish and sea-birds. It seems a reasonable guess that they first settled

in Village Bay on the south-east coast of Hirta. Sheltered, with a good beach, plenty of water and an infinite supply of stone for building, it was the obvious place. But there is no doubt that a large and early settlement also existed in Gleann Mor at the less attractive north end of the island, where there are cultivation ridges and the remains of sixteen ancient structures. Because of their remoteness from Village Bay, where the latter-day St Kildans lived, these are reasonably well preserved. Each structure consists of three or four beehive chambers clustered around a circular open court with a narrow gateway, upon which two dry stone walls converge like horns. Although for one reason or another this settlement was probably deserted at an early date, from the 18th century onwards its buildings were used by the St Kildans as summer shielings. They would pen calves and lambs in the horned courts, milk the ewes and cows, and sometimes spend the night in the beehive chambers, which they had to crawl into through doors little more than 1 foot 6 inches square.

The most important of the structures in Gleann Mor, known also as the Female Warrior's Glen, was christened by Martin, the Amazon's House. The Amazon appears to have been a principal figure in St Kildan mythology, but unfortunately Martin decided against recording any of the traditions concerning her for fear of boring his readers, though he did describe the house in which she is supposed to have lived : 'The body of this house contains not above nine persons sitting; there are three beds or low vaults at the side of the wall, which contains five men each, and are separated by a pillar; at the entry to one of these low vaults is a stone standing upon one end; upon this stone she is reported ordinarily to have laid her helmet; there are two stones on the other side, upon which she is said to have laid her sword.' Since Martin's time many of the stones have been removed to build cleits but the bones of the structure remain. There are also a number of menhirs and stone circles close by the house, which suggest that it may have been a place of religious significance.

The Amazon loved hunting and since in her day, it seems, there was dry land between St Kilda and the Outer Hebrides, she used to set her hounds after the deer and chase them across to Harris and Lewis. As if to corroborate this, Martin records that some time before his arrival in St Kilda a large pair of antlers had been found on the top of Oiseval buried a foot below the ground and with them a wooden bowl full of deer's grease. Although nothing more is known of the St Kildan Amazon, there exists in the traditions of

Harris a long and involved legend of a female warrior, who used
to hunt over the dry land between the Long Island and St Kilda,
and who is probably the same person. The story of the Amazon,
however fragmentary, and perhaps for this very reason, has fired
imaginations and brought forth theories on the origins of early
St Kildan society, from the suggestion that the island was first inhabited by a matriarchal society, to the wilder fancy that it was once
part of the lost continent of Atlantis. Although there can be no
doubt that a very long time ago St Kilda was part of a larger land
mass, and it is a possibility that, much later, deer and even hunting
tribes may have roamed across it, the house of the Amazon and
the other beehive structures in Gleann Mor probably belong to
the Stone or even the Iron Age, though the Amazon herself may
predate them.

In the 17th century there were several primitive dwellings
on Boreray, most of which have since disappeared, though one can
still see cultivation ridges, suggesting that the early settlers probably
lived there too, at least during the summer months. The most important of the buildings on Boreray was undoubtedly the Stallir
House, traces of which are visible today. Martin described it as
being 'much larger than that of the female warrior in St Kilda, but
of the same model in all respects; it is all green without like a little
hill; the inhabitants there have a tradition that it was built by one
Stallir, who was a devout hermit of St Kilda'. According to another
tradition Stallir, also known as the Man of the Rocks, led a rebellion against the steward and, taking his followers with him, left the
main island and went to live on Boreray, where he built himself a
large house. It was a circular building, mostly underground, with
a corbelled roof and a central chamber with room enough for
sixteen people to sit around the open fireplace in the middle of the
floor. Let into the walls were six apartment beds, each of which
could accommodate several bodies packed in sardine style, head to
tail. The beds were connected by a passage so that it was
possible to pass from one to another without going into the central
chamber. Many of them had names—the largest was called Rastalla
or the leading Climber's Bed, the smallest Leaba nan Con or the
Dog's Bed—though these may have been added much later. The
door was called Bar Kigh.

The stones used to build Stallir House were supposed to have
been of the same type as those used in the construction of the fort
on Dun. According to the Rev Kenneth Macaulay they were very
large and nearly square, as if they had been quarried, and, because

of their colour and kind, could not possibly have been found in St Kilda. All that remains of the fort today, is a section of wall covered in lichen, and though the stones are a respectable size there seems to be no reason why they should not have come from the island. The fort, which is the only relic of war in St Kilda, is situated in a strategic position near the tip of the Dun overlooking the Bay, though it is difficult to see that it could have served any useful purpose, since the absence of water on Dun would have made it unsuitable even as a place of refuge. It is said to have been built by the Fir Bolg, a Celtic warrior tribe from pre-Christian Ireland.

The mythology of the Celtic invasions of Ireland was formalized in the 8th century AD by learned monks of the early Christian church. Wishing to preserve the traditions of their pagan past, but not its religions, the monks divided up the arrival of their ancestors into a series of invasions, the last of which was supposed to confer Christian respectability on the Irish Celts. One of the earlier and more authentic invasions was led by the Fir Bolg, originally a race of agriculturalists from Greece. They were defeated by the next wave of invaders, the Tuatha Dé Danann, at the battle of Moytura and forced to live in Connaught and the outer Irish islands. It was from here that they may have invaded and even colonized St Kilda, though a popular tradition among the later inhabitants held that the first Celtic colony on the island was founded by an Irish reiver called Mac Quin.

Whether these Celtic invaders assimilated the original Neolithic inhabitants or drove them off is not known; they may even have found the island deserted and started a new settlement in Village Bay. The Gleann Mor settlement was abandoned about this time, possibly because of the Celts, but more likely due to a loss of fertility in the arable land. Neolithic farmers had no knowledge of husbandry and tended simply to move elsewhere when the soil became infertile. Such a move, if it happened, may well have coincided with the gradual subordination of farming to hunting as the climate deteriorated and St Kilda, of necessity, became a bird culture. But there is some evidence, in the shape of an earth dyke marking a boundary line across the top of the glen, which suggests that for a time at least the Gleann Mor settlement was coeval with the settlement in Village Bay.

Although life on Hirta probably continued much as it had done in the past and was to do in the future, the Celts undoubtedly initiated some changes and helped to mould a more distinctive St Kildan culture by the introduction of new ideas. They brought

other gods and priests to go with them. Stallir, described in the
Christian tradition as a 'devout hermit', was probably a Druid.
Nearby the Stallir House on Boreray there was 'a large circle of
huge stones fixed perpendicularly in the ground, at equal distances
from one another, with one more remarkably regular in the centre
which is flat in the top and one would think sacred in a more
eminent degree'. In all Macaulay mentions five such altars in St
Kilda and entertains a long discourse on the probability of there
having been Druids on the island. Certainly their influence was
felt in many of the Western Isles, especially Lewis, and there is no
real reason why it should not have reached St Kilda. Macaulay's
only doubt is instigated by the absence of the ritual oak and mistletoe on the island, though he suggests that the Druids could possibly
have operated without them. As pollen analysis has shown at one
time oak trees did in fact grow there, though of mistletoe there is
no evidence. Toland, an 18th-century author of a history of the
Druids, who evidently had read Martin but never visited St Kilda,
shared Macaulay's views with enthusiasm. He believed firmly that
not only was Stallir a Druid on Boreray, but that the Amazon on
Hirta was in fact a Druidess. He conjectured that Druid and
Druidess were probably 'not unacquainted' with each other, which
somehow opens up startling perspectives.

Very little is known about the Druids and the religion of the pre-
Christian Celts, but they left a spiritual legacy of lasting influence.
Their central belief in a form of metempsychosis, which filled the
natural world with souls and spirits, became deeply engrained in
the Celtic character especially in those remote areas of the West,
where man's struggle for survival in a harsh environment involved
him so completely with the elemental. St Kilda was no exception
and in spite of the untiring efforts of missionaries in the 19th
century the islanders never really lost what had become their
natural religion. When Alexander Buchan came to St Kilda in
1705 as the island's first missionary he found that Martin in his
alter ego of avenging Knox, had tried during his three-week visit
to rid the St Kildans of some of their ancient religious practices
and made them overthrow several of their altars and stone circles.
Buchan observed that although some idolatrous monuments of a
physical nature had been destroyed, 'the spiritual ones which were
erected in the hearts of the islanders were not touched'.

During the 6th and 7th centuries islands off the coasts of Ireland
and Britain began to be sought out by early Christians as sites for
monasteries and religious settlements. The more isolated they were,

the better they suited the purpose of those monks and anchorites, who were less concerned with converting heathens than pursuing an ideal, defined as 'seeking the place of one's resurrection', and leading a life of solitude within a religous community, but away from the rest of the world. St Kilda was ideally suited to this kind of religious activity, though presuming that the island was still inhabited, some missionary work would have been inevitable.

At one time there were three churches on the island, Christ Church, St Columba's and St Brendan's, but now there is little trace left of any of them. Christ Church, the largest of the three, measuring 24 feet by 14 feet, was built of stone and in 1697 had a thatched roof. It was too small to hold the entire congregation, most of whom had to stand in the churchyard during services. St Brendan's church lay a mile to the south-west of the village on the lower slopes of Ruaival. According to Macaulay, 'It has an altar within, and some monkish cells without it. These are almost entire and must of consequence be of later date, than the holy places dedicated to Christ and Columba.' A plethora of churches on so small an island invited the theory that the population of St Kilda must have been much larger in its earlier history. Dr Johnson, however, referring to the great quantity of religious remains to be found throughout the Western Isles, aptly remarked, 'These venerable fragments do not prove the people of former times to have been more numerous but to have been more devout.'

If the three churches of St Kilda, which were probably no larger than ordinary houses of their period, do not necessarily suggest a populace of enthusiastic converts, they do give at least presumptive evidence of a monastic settlement on the island. Inevitably the founding of an ascetic community in St Kilda has often been attributed to St Columba himself, or failing him, at least to one of his disciples. The ascription is supported by Columba's tendency to call the churches he built either after Christ or the Trinity; and by a well on Hirta called Toberi Clerich—the Clerk was the familiar name by which St Columba was known throughout the West; but it seems unlikely that Columba's political interests would have allowed him to spend time in anywhere quite so remote as St Kilda.

The unusual degree of isolation enjoyed by the people of Hirta did not, however, safeguard them from the Vikings, who destroyed so many island sanctuaries between the 8th and 10th centuries. Whether the religious community came to an end with the advent of the Norsemen is not known, but if this was the case the Christian ethos had already worked itself into the structure of island life and

was not to be dislodged. Where Druidism had given a ritual form
to the St Kildan's relationship with nature, early Christianity had
done the same for his relationship with his fellow islanders. The
ordering of social life on Hirta in the centuries to come, from the
marriage laws to the sharing of the bird harvest, was to be based
on the example set by the early Christian community, which with
Celtic flexibility had no doubt simply redefined in Christian terms
whatever system was already in existence. As late as the 19th
century the religious beliefs of the islanders were being described
as a mixture of Druidism and early Christianity : their social organization might well have been described in terms of a similar combination of necessity and law.

The influence of the Vikings on St Kilda is difficult to assess. A
number of boat-shaped Viking graves and other structures possibly
of Norse origin suggest a settlement of some kind, most likely a
base for supplying the long ships with water and food. They may
even have introduced sheep to the island of Soay for this purpose.
But how long they stayed and whether the Celtic population survived them, is at present impossible to tell. From the earliest physical
descriptions of St Kildans it would seem that the blond Nordic
type predominated, but probably no more than on some of the
other Hebridean islands.

As was the case with most places they visited the Vikings were not
remembered kindly in St Kildan lore. The following story is one of
the rare examples of the islanders failing their reputation for
hospitality.

The king of Lochlainn or Norway, who was a popular figure in
Gaelic mythology, had several sons, one of whom happened to be
sailing in St Kilda waters when his ship struck a rock off the
southernmost point of Soay and was wrecked. Despite the heavy
seas he managed to get ashore on Hirta and being exhausted and
thirsty was delighted to find a well of pure, sweet water with which
to refresh himself. He bent down over the pool to have a drink but
was so intent on this purpose that he failed to see mirrored in its
surface a band of wild-looking St Kildans creeping up on him.
They jumped him from behind and held his head under water
until he was drowned. The skerry on which his ship is said to have
foundered was called after him, the Rock of the Son of the King
of Norway.

The chief legacy of the Norsemen may well have been linguistic. In
1758 Macaulay remarked how 'the St Kildans speak a very corrupt

dialect of the Galic, adulterated with a little mixture of the Norwegian tongue', though by the end of the 19th century the differences had mostly been eradicated, and only place names still recalled Viking influence. Wherever the long ships ventured on the west coast of Scotland, features of land which could be seen from the sea as a rule received Norse names, while the names of inland sites remained Gaelic. In St Kilda names like Oiseval (Norse for 'east hill'), Soay (Norse for 'sheep isle') and Boreray (Norse for 'north isle') all refer to points easily seen from the Viking ships. The names of glens, corries, streams and rocks are mostly Gaelic, though, as might be expected, the exceptions to the rule are numerous. Dun, An Torc, Mullach Bi may all be seen from the sea but are Gaelic, while (Tober) Childa, the name of a spring on Hirta, is Norse.

The word 'Childa' is still believed by many to be the true etymon of the name St Kilda. There is no record of a saint called Kilda, though Martin and others simply assumed that he or she must have existed, but since at one time it was common practice in the West to name wells and springs after saints, the canonization of 'Childa' could easily have occurred by mistake. Or it could have happened in another way. The word 'Kilda' first appears in writing on a map dated 1588, but without the prefix 'Saint'. This may have become attached in the 17th century through an error of Dutch cartographers, who possibly confused Hirta with another island nearer to the west coast of the outer Hebrides originally called 'Skildar'. One etymology of St Kilda suggests that it derives from the word Culdees (Celi De—Companion of God), who were a movement of anchorites thought by some to have been the first Christian settlers in St Kilda. Another theory makes out a case for Kilda being a corruption of the word Hirta by the islanders themselves, who tended to pronounce 'r' as 'l' which gave 'Hilta', becoming 'Kilta', but since the islanders were rarely heard to use any other name for the island than Hirta it seems an unlikely explanation.

The same controversy exists over the etymology of Hirta. Some say it is a Celtic word meaning 'gloom or death', others that it derives from the Gaelic 'h-Iar-Tir' meaning 'westland'. Both theories are supported by the same myth of an island of spirits beyond the western horizon where the dead go, for which Hirta could well have been mistaken. Another derivation somehow managed to wrest Hirta from the Latin 'terra', giving the excuse that to the islanders Hirta was the entire world, their earth. More convincing is the explanation taken from an Icelandic Saga, which, in an account of a voyage from Iceland to Ireland in 1202, mentions a visit to some 'islands that are called Hirtir'. Hirtir is the plural of the Norse word 'hjortr', meaning 'a stag' and if one considers the shape of Hirta, taking the Dun on one side and the Cambir and Soay on the other as antlers, and the remainder of the island as the head, the resemblance to a stag is fair.

The first description of St Kilda, though little more than a passing reference, sounds a romantic note of loneliness, which was to resound throughout its written history. It comes in John of Fordun's *Scotichronicon*, compiled *c.* 1380 in which he mentions 'the isle of Irte, which is agreed to be under the Circius and on the margine of the world, beyond which there is found no land in these bounds'.

A fuller account of St Kilda was given by Donald Monro in his *Descriptione of the Western Iles of Scotland callit Hybrides*. Monro, who was High Dean of the Isles, travelled through most of the Hebrides in 1549. Although he may not have visited St Kilda he manages to give a convincing description of the island and appears to have formed from somewhere a low opinion of its inhabitants, whom he describes as 'simple poor people, scarce learnit in aney religioun', though as High Dean and a missionary, Monro was doubtless a stern judge. He also relates how MacLeod's steward had once taken some malt across to St Kilda and brewed it up for the natives to drink, with the perhaps intended result that 'baith men, weemen and bairns were deid drunken, sua that they could not stand on their feet'. Whether Monro includes this anecdote for its moral significance or simply because he finds it amusing is not evident. The steward, who today might easily be placed in that same category as the white man who sold fire water to the Indians, comes in for no adverse criticism. He describes how 'the said steward receives their dewties in meill and reistit mutton, wyld foullis reistit and selchis', and mentions that he also acted as priest and was responsible for baptizing the children, though if he did not turn up the islanders would do the job themselves. Monro ends his account on a more lyrical note : 'In this faire Ile is faire sheip, falcon nests and wyld fouls biggand, but the streams of the sea ar starke, and ar verey eivill or entring in aney of the saidis iles.'

Few and brief as they are, many of the early accounts of St Kilda were drawn from the same uncertain sources and went over the same sparse ground, with remarks on the island's inaccessibility, the activities of the steward, the ignorance of the natives and the peculiarities of the sheep. Bishop Leslie in a 16th century history of Scotland, which includes a reference to Hirta, states that Soay was uninhabited except by very wild sheep, which were not like sheep at all; but elsewhere he compares the more ordinary sheep on Hirta to buffaloes, which could be taken as a threat to his credibility. A description of the Western Isles, written towards the end of the 16th century, mentions the absence of horses in St Kilda, adding that strangers never visited the island and that its barbarous inhabitants were not even clever enough to catch fish, though another account of the same period implies that the islanders did not need to catch fish since Hirta was so rich in corn, cattle, sheep and seabirds.

It is not until Martin's visit in 1697 that detailed information about St Kilda and its inhabitants first becomes available. The early history, if history is not too presumptuous a word, remains a blankish page lightly pencilled over with guesswork. Some of it, perhaps, will be filled in, when the archaeological secrets of the island are at length revealed; but the gaps will always be large and the story of antiquity in this strange and distant place will always be obscured by those ambient white mists of its own creation.

CHAPTER THREE

Ownership, Rent and Economy

'So long as it remains out of touch with the rest of the world an ideal society can be a viable society.'

ALDOUS HUXLEY, *Island*

The first owner of St Kilda won the island in a race, or so runs the legend. It tells of a contest between the MacLeods of Harris and the MacDonalds of Uist, who both claimed the island for their own. To settle the dispute the contenders agreed to a boat-race from a certain point on the Long Island across fifty miles of open sea to St Kilda. It was stipulated that the two boats were to be of the same size and type, crewed by an equal number of men, and that the first person to touch land on Hirta would be declared the winner and secure possession of the island for his clan and chief.

The race was close, but as the two birlinns rounded the upper lip of Village Bay within yards of the cliffs of Oiseval the MacDonald boat drew ahead by a few lengths. Assured of losing, the exhausted MacLeods had almost given up hope, when one of the crew, a young man called Coll MacLeod, threw down his oar and rushed forward into the bows of the boat. Drawing his sword he severed his left hand and with a triumphant cry hurled it over the heads of the MacDonalds. The hand sailed through the air, describing a momentary arc of blood against the sky, and landed on a rocky promontory, thereby winning the race and its coveted prize for the MacLeods.

The story may have some truth in it—a red hand in a MacLeod coat of arms is said to commemorate Coll's gallant action—but it seems more likely that the MacLeods acquired St Kilda in less dramatic circumstances. John of Islay, who was Lord of the Isles, is known to have made a present of a number of islands including St Kilda, to his son Reginald *c.* 1360. From Reginald the island passed to the MacDonalds of Sleat, who may simply have sold it to the MacLeods of Dunvegan. Although it was owned by different branches of the family St Kilda remained a MacLeod island for 500 years until after the evacuation in 1930.

For most of this long tenure the MacLeods managed St Kilda through a tacksman or steward, as was the common practice in the highlands and islands of Scotland until the middle of the 18th century. Tacksmen, who were usually relatives of the chief, held their lands from him in return for a fixed rent and a promise to provide a certain number of fighting men. After the '45 rebellion, when the power of the clans diminished and the old order of tacksmen began to disintegrate, the straightforward system of barter and payment in kind, which up until then had dominated the economic life of the highlands, was gradually replaced by a money economy. The MacLeods, whose estates included many distant and secluded islands, were slow to adapt to this new arrangement; and in St Kilda, where the people lived in almost complete isolation from the mainland, money was not introduced until the second half of the 19th century.

As the world of the mainland changed, as new industries developed and power shifted to the towns and old allegiances altered irrevocably, life on St Kilda remained the same. The islanders continued to worship MacLeod from afar as a kind of tribal deity; and their economy, despite late efforts to bring it up to date, remained primitive. The MacLeods were criticized for allowing the St Kildans to fall behind the times and even accused of encouraging them to do so in order to exploit them more easily. But the task of modernizing St Kilda was far from simple, and in the last hundred years of the community's existence, when these accusations were mostly levelled, the island had become more of a liability to its owners than an asset. Certainly there were some bad landlords who extracted exorbitant rents from the islands, but in difficult circumstances most of the MacLeods appear to have been fair and reasonable proprietors.

The affairs of the St Kildans were handled almost entirely by the steward or tacksman appointed by MacLeod. He himself visited the island rarely, if ever, though he always retained ultimate responsibility and power over its inhabitants. Latterly the steward or factor, as he came to be known, was an employee of MacLeod acting purely on his behalf, but in earlier times he was often a member of a cadet branch of the family and held St Kilda on a lease from his Chief. He had to pay a rental for the island, but after he had collected the rent from the St Kildans, as long as the value of their produce was widely recognized, he could usually expect to make a profit.

The tenancy of St Kilda involved a yearly visit to the island for two or three weeks in the summer to see to the wants of the islanders and collect their rents. If, after the rent had been paid, there was a surplus, the steward would use it to buy basic necessities such as seed corn, barley or oats for the St Kildans, which he would bring out on his next visit. But in a thin year, if the crops failed or the bird harvest was poor, he risked making a loss. On such occasions the islanders were at the mercy of the steward, who, if he was unscrupulous, might attempt to make good his deficit at their expense. One winter during the 17th century the islanders were reduced to eating seaweed because the steward had taken all their food supplies. But the St Kildans were not incapable of standing up for their rights and when this same steward decided to extract a sheep from every family on the island as a new form of taxation, they refused to give them up. The steward went away without the sheep but dispatched his brother with a large number of men to take them off by force. The St Kildans, however, armed with knives and fishing rods, attacked their oppressors and drove them from the island, telling them to take a message back to the steward that they had no intention of paying any new taxes.

When Martin visited St Kilda in 1697 he went with the steward's party, which consisted of sixty men, whom the islanders had to support during their three week stay : 'The steward lives upon the charge of the inhabitants until the time that the solan geese are ready to fly, which the inhabitants think long enough.' This ancient due, known as 'cuddiche', whereby members of the Chief's household had to be given food and shelter anywhere on his lands, was still levied on St Kilda long after it had died out elsewhere. According to Martin, however, the numbers in the steward's retinue were soon to be reduced and other 'ancient and unreasonable exactions', such as the two treats of all the milk on the island which the steward's men received, once on arrival and again on St Columba's day, were to be done away with. The steward's retinue was largely made up of sick men from Dunvegan, 'the most meagre in the parish', who were carried over to St Kilda 'to be recruited with good chear'. Evidently the example of rude health and physical strength enjoyed by the St Kildans, the plentiful food and good water to be had free, and perhaps a superstitious belief in the magical power of this far western island, made it an ideal spa.

During the steward's absence from the island, his affairs were looked after by a ground-officer, an islander elected by the others but subject to approval by the steward. Since the officer represented both the interests of the St Kildans and those of the steward every family on the island took the precaution of paying him a measure of barley each year 'to maintain his character'. Despite these and other financial rewards it was not a particularly enviable job. The officer was given the questionable honour of leading fowling expeditions to the other islands and stacs and of being the first to leap from the boat on to the rocks when a tricky landing had to be made. It was also his duty to preside over debates and to make sure that any decision taken by lots was carried out fairly.

His most important function was to lead all discussions among the islanders about the payment of the rent and, when the time came, to dispute it in every last detail with the steward. If there was any disagreement the officer was not allowed to give in until he had either won his point or put the steward into such a rage that the latter gave him three blows with a cudgel on the crown of his head. If he only irritated the steward to the extent of one or two blows, the unfortunate officer had to persevere until he had received the full quota of three. By the end of the 17th century this custom was already dying out and Martin was told by the steward that, anyway, if he were really to get angry with the officer, he would not confine himself to three blows.

When there was a serious disagreement between the steward and the St Kildans, the officer was finally responsible to his fellow islanders. On such occasions he was expected to travel to Skye and make a formal representation of their case before MacLeod at Dunvegan Castle. Here, according to Martin, he 'makes his entry very submissively, taking off his bonnet at a great distance when he appears in Mack-Leod's presence, bowing his head and hand low near to the ground, his retinue doing the like behind him one after another, making, as it were, a chain'. His retinue was made up of the crew of the St Kilda boat, who were there to make absolutely sure that the officer represented their interests and not those of the steward. There was always the danger that he might have accepted a bribe. As it was, his job entitled him to an extra acre or two of land and the privilege of keeping the steward's bonnet when he was away from the island. His wife was equally graced with the 'kerch' or headdress of the steward's wife, as well as an ounce of indigo. But in return for these modest perks the officer had to entertain the steward during his stay on Hirta and provide him with a large barley cake, baked in the shape of a triangle, at every meal;

on Sundays he also had to make sure that there was either beef or mutton served at his table for the steward's enjoyment. On the whole the advantages and inconveniences of the officer's job were evenly balanced.

After survival the main goal of the St Kildan community was to produce enough goods to pay the rent. It could be argued that the extra pressure which this brought to bear, not only kept the island populated but made it prosper. For most of its history St Kilda was a self-supporting commonwealth with an economy suited to the terms of its own isolation. Imports were kept down to a few basic necessities and although there was some direct trading with other islands in the Outer Hebrides it was restricted by the dangers of the sea-voyage. Almost all the island's trade was done through MacLeod or his steward, who collected the produce, sold it on the mainland and, after subtracting the rent, bought for the St Kildans whatever they required. The system worked well as long as there was a demand for St Kilda produce and as long as the islanders did not need to import more than they could export. Towards the end of the 19th century, however, these conditions ceased to be fulfilled. Under pressure to introduce reforms MacLeod encouraged the islanders to sell their produce independently on the mainland, but they lacked the organization and initiative to carry the venture through, preferring the old system, where the responsibility of finding markets and the costs of transportation were borne by MacLeod.

The economy of St Kilda was based on the produce of sea-birds; and although cattle, sheep, wool, tweed, tallow, cheese, barley, corn and fish were also exported in quantities which varied considerably according to supply and demand, the prime wealth of the island lay in the oil, feathers and dried carcases of gannets, fulmar and puffins. Until the end of the 18th century barley and corn were almost as important an export as sea-birds but in later years, due partly to inefficient land use, cereal production began to drop and by 1850 the St Kildans were not producing enough grain even for their own needs. Sea-bird produce, however, continued as the staple, and for most of the 19th century gannet and fulmar oil was sold on the mainland for medicinal purposes and for heating and lighting; fulmar and puffin feathers for stuffing cheap mattresses; and dried fulmar or young gannets for food. But towards the end of the century the demand for these products fell away and the St Kildan economy, unable to adapt to the changing needs of the modern world, collapsed. The islanders were able to make a little money from tourists and from selling tweed, which by 1900 had become the only St Kildan product of any value to the outside world, but neither tweed nor tourists brought in enough to save the situation. As exports went down the list of imports lengthened, until it included articles such as tea, whisky, sugar, salt, paraffin, corn, meal, seed, tools, tobacco, hardware and furniture. The island was no longer self-supporting, and, as the trade deficit grew, the St Kildans came to rely more and more on charity for survival.

The rent, which accounted for most if not all of the island's surplus produce, was usually a composite amount calculated on the number of crofts, sheep and cows owned by the St Kildans. In 1883 they were paying £2 per croft, 7s per cow and 9d per sheep, which came to £95 all told; two years later the rent had to be reduced to nearer £60 to suit the islanders' poorer pockets. If necessary MacLeod was prepared to make changes in the system. When, for instance the people complained at having to pay rent on a fixed number of sheep (some owned more than others), he readily altered the arrangement so that each man only paid rent on his own sheep; but the islanders continued to be notoriously forgetful about the actual numbers of sheep in their possession. In later years the St Kildans often fell behind with the payment of the rent, but they were never subjected to harassment.

Like the need to survive, the responsibility for paying the rent was shared by the community as a whole and all property on the island which served these twin purposes belonged to the public. Pasture, arable land, cliffs, boats, cleits and fowling ropes were all held in common, but at the same time scrupulously divided up into different sized plots and portions among the island's families. Each family contributed towards the rent according to the amount of land and the number of cattle and sheep that it owned. The arable land, which was divided up into hundreds of little strips, was parcelled out among the families by the St Kilda parliament for three-year periods. After three years it was redistributed, but the amount of land owned by each family usually remained the same. As with most primitive economic systems which can be called communistic, there was no simple principle of share and share alike in St Kilda, but an intricate web of ownership rights delimited by a set of rules based on kinship, residence and the primary ownership of arable land. Whatever the individual rights of a St Kildan, however, they were always subject to the overweening rights of his kin group and the community as a whole.

Imports and Exports (F. Thompson)

Prices of Exports 1799–1902

1799 A sheep   3s 6d
      A cow   30s
      Feathers   3s per stone (sold in the Hebrides for 10s per stone)
1831 A cow   25s 6d
      A pony   25s
1842 Feathers   5s per stone (sold on the mainland for 15s per stone)
1875 A cow   £3
      Tallow   6s 6d per stone
      Cheese   6s per stone
      Ling   7d each
      Cod   3d each
      Bream   1d each
      Black feathers   6s per stone
      Grey feathers   5s per stone
      Fulmar oil   5s per pint
1877 Cheese   6s 6d per stone
1885 Tweed   3s per yell
      Blankets   2s 6d per yell
1902 Fulmar Oil   6d per pint (later $4\frac{1}{2}$d per pint)

Prices of Imports 1877

      Meal   25s per boll
      Oats   25s per boll
      Salt   3s per cwt
      Sugar   7d per lb
      Tea   5s per lb
      Whisky   4s per bottle
      Tobacco   5s per lb
      Leather (soles)   2s per lb
      Leather (uppers)   2s 3d per lb
      Bonnets (for men)   4s each
      Cravats   3s each

            St Kilda stone = 24 English lbs
            St Kilda pint = 5 English pints

All other divisions of property were made according to the amount of arable land owned. For instance, when the cliffs (where the young fulmar were caught on their nests) were divided into lots, a family which owned a large area of land received a proportionate amount of cliff; but since some sections of cliff provided more nesting places than others, the location of the cliff-lot was often more important than its size. For this reason the cliff-lots were redistributed every year.

The cliffs on Hirta and the Dun were divided into lots so that each family might be responsible for protecting the breeding ledges in their own section of cliff from interference by sheep, dogs and black-backed gulls. In August, when the young fulmar were taken from their nests, each family would harvest its own ledges. If a man fell ill, or for some other reason could not take part in the harvest, his work would be done for him : where necessary, help was always forthcoming. After the fulmar had been gathered all the birds were put together, then redistributed between the families, allowances being made for the old people and the sick. Any young fulmar caught 'off the nest' were not subject to division because, since they would otherwise almost certainly have been taken by blackbacks or hoodie crows, they were regarded as saved and therefore the rightful property of their deliverers. Because of the different fowling techniques involved, the cliffs of Boreray, Soay and their stacs were not divided up into lots, though the birds caught there were distributed among the families in the usual way.

'They are very exact in their properties,' wrote Martin in 1697, 'and divide both the fishing, as well as fowling rocks with as great niceness as they do their corn and grass. One will not allow his neighbour to fish and sit on his seat, for this being a part of his possession, he will take care that no encroachment be made upon the least part of it; and this with a particular regard to their successors, that they may lose no privilege depending upon any parcel of their farm.' Even the boat was divided up into sections among all the families on the island, the size of the individual portions again varying according to the amount of land owned. When they went out in the boat to catch fish for the rent, the catch would be distributed among all the families, but if the fish was for their own consumption only the families of those who took part in the expedition would receive a share. When they fished from the rocks every man fished for himself.

Pasture was held in common without separate rights, but not so the flock nor the herd. The number of sheep and cattle owned by a family could vary within certain agreed parameters; and where a family owned more or less livestock than another it contributed to the payment of the rent accordingly. If a family lost a sheep, whether by accident or disease, the loss was indemnified by the

others. When the accident had been the fault of another islander
the rule was quite simply a sheep for a sheep. But if, for instance,
the wind had blown an animal over a cliff, its owner was given a
replacement by one of the wealthier families, who took it in turns
to compensate such losses.

Many of the principles upon which the St Kildan commonwealth
was based may have been inherited from the early Christian community, but since on the whole the island laws provided an adaptive and efficient means to survival for a small and isolated society,
they may have been operating for much longer. The St Kildans
knew and abided by the Mosaic Law, but as there was next to no
crime on the island, laws were mostly concerned with the division
of property and the administration of justice in sharing. When they
arose disputes were settled, if agreement could not be reached
through discussion, by casting lots and in the final count by swearing
an oath in public on a small brass crucifix. It was assumed that this
last resort completely excluded the possibility of either party telling
a lie. If an argument ever came to blows an islander might be fined
2s in kind for beating his neighbour and up to 4s 6d if he drew
blood. Serious offences such as these were usually noted by the
officer who explained the circumstances to the steward on his yearly
visit. The steward would then pass judgement and decide whether
or not to exact the fine. Nearly all aspects of life on the island were
thus governed by laws of one kind or another and as much time
was spent in discussing their infinite detail as in administering them.
As Martin observed, 'There is not a parcel of men in the world
more scrupulously nice and punctilious in maintaining their liber-
ties and properties than these are, being most religiously fond of
their ancient laws and statutes.'

Decisions on all matters concerning the welfare of the community
were taken by the Mòd, or the St Kilda Parliament, as it later came
to be known—a deliberative assembly composed of all the grown
males on the island. The members met every morning except Sunday outside one of the houses in the street, and sat around in all
weathers on top of dykes, wind-breaks or on the ground to discuss a
wide range of topics. The officer supposedly acted as speaker but
there was little order and everybody spoke at once, which made
things rather lively. The most important function of the parliament
was to decide what work should be done that day and how it should
be approached. If a job needed doing urgently, during harvest-time
for instance, little time would be lost in discussion and the parliament would quickly adjourn so that the men could get on with it;

but on days when there was no particular rush they might spend
the whole day just talking. The crucial moment came towards midday, when, if the parliament was still sitting, the decision had to
be taken whether it was worth doing any work in the afternoon, now
that the morning was already gone. Often enough they would
return after lunch to continue the debate.

Stories, myths, sagas, tales of bravery on the cliffs, famous fowling incidents also found their way on to the agenda, though by the
19th century they had been replaced by long and detailed accounts
of visits to the mainland or discussions about the last steamer load
of tourists. Nor was the parliament above hearing the island's
gossip and examining the various family relationships and, latterly,
feuds, which were of current interest. But for all that the St Kilda
Parliament was a serious institution. It supervised the payment of
the rent, the allocation of property, the testing of fowling ropes,
and while it saw to such relatively minor details as the equitable distribution of puffin eggs, it regularly took life and death decisions
(for instance, on if and when it was safe for the boat to go out),
which might affect the existence of the entire community. As old as
the community itself, and as necessary to its survival as the body
of island laws which it represented, the parliament ensured that no
man was raised above another and that all shared the common
wealth or want, as the case might be.

Satisfied with their own arrangement the St Kildans never regis-
tered a vote which helped send a man to Westminster. Nor did they
pay taxes, since it was not worth anybody's while to collect them,
and the benefits of taxation never reached their shores. In Martin's
time, however, there were two island taxes, which were known respectively as the fire-penny and the pot-penny. The former existed
because there was only one tinder-box on the island, which the
owner charged for the use of every time a fire had to be lit. On Hirta
this was a rare event since the fires in the houses were kept burning continuously. But if an expedition set out for Soay or Boreray,
the steel and tinder had to be taken along, whereupon the owner
received three eggs or a small sea-bird from each person as payment. Martin claimed to have abolished the fire-penny, much to
the delight of the St Kildans (who thought it an unreasonable form
of extortion), by showing them how to make a spark with a knife
and a crystal. The pot-penny was a less objectionable levy, whereby
anyone who lent their cooking-pot for the use of the members of
an expedition to one of the other islands or stacs, received insurance

against the possibility of the pot being smashed. Since every household owned a pot there was no danger of a monopoly.

Marriage in St Kilda until the end of the 17th century was celebrated in the simplest of fashions. The islanders married when they were very young; the bride was not usually more than thirteen or fourteen, the groom only a little older. When a couple wanted to get married the officer or the steward, if he happened to be on the island at the time, called all the people together by the church and read the banns. If there were no objections the couple straight away swore an oath of fidelity on the crucifix, which they both held in their right hands, and were declared married. After this sensibly brief ceremony the rest of the day and night were devoted to feasting, singing and dancing.

Before a young St Kildan could get married, however, he had to demonstrate that he was capable of supporting a wife and a family by giving a display of his courage and skill as a cragsman. Near the top of Ruaival on the south-west coast of Hirta there is a natural arch in the rock known as the Mistress Stone. It is formed by a great slab of gabbro which juts out from the side of the hill and rests upon a pinnacle of the cliff. The uppermost surface of the stone is quite flat and it was on its extreme edge, overlooking an almost sheer drop of 250 feet to the sea below, that the prospective candidate for marriage had to show his worth. Observed by his friends and his betrothed he had to stand on the lip of the stone, as it were the end of a gangplank, and balancing upon the heel of one foot, bend forwards and grasp the other foot with both hands. He had to hold this position, looking down at the rocks and surf below him, until his friends decided that he had proved himself.

A difficult feat to perform at all times, but almost impossible if there was a wind blowing, the ritual of the Mistress Stone was discontinued by the latter-day St Kildans. But in Martin's time there is no doubt that some form of rite did take place and that it was extremely dangerous. Although they could easily have cheated by facing another way and performing the antic over a drop of a mere seven feet to the path below the arch, it would have been out of character with the islanders' pride in their prowess as cragsmen. When Martin, who was far from cowardly, was asked if he would like to try his luck on the Mistress Stone, he refused outright, not being prepared to lose his life and his mistress in the same moment.

In time the St Kildans came around to his way of thinking.

With a smaller population and more women than men on the island the life of a young man became too valuable to the community to be risked so pointlessly. During the course of the 19th century the bias of marriage gradually shifted until the burden of proof lay with the women, for whom the fear of not finding a husband often became obsessive. The price of failure was not so final as a fall over the cliffs, but many considered the life of a spinster in St Kilda to be a fate worse by far.

The succinct marriage ceremony of Martin's time was later replaced by a more drawn-out and less joyful celebration. A week or so before the wedding the Reiteach, or contract, was held in the house of the bride's father. The male relatives and friends of the young couple were invited to drink a solemn toast to the coming occasion. A single glass of whisky was passed round from hand to hand. No women were allowed to be present and conversation was kept low and to a minimum.

The officer had by this time been relieved of his duties by the island's minister, who conducted a conventional marriage service in the church, complete with sermon, though instead of a ring a piece of woollen thread was used as a token of betrothal. The wedding feast, too, had become a solemn occasion, no longer accompanied by singing and dancing. The Reverend Neil Mac-Kenzie, who was minister in St Kilda from 1829–43, gives an eye-witness account:

'As soon as they were married they (the couple) went home; and we saw no more of them till after tea, when the governor of the feast, the bride's brother, came, dressed, in the uniform (which is a rag of white cotton cloth sewed to each shoulder and the front of his bonnet), to invite us to the marriage feast. . . . When we went we found every man in the island seated in the house of the bride's father, with a table of planks before them; the ground served them for seats. One end of the board was raised much higher; this was intended for us, with a chest for a seat, and opposite to us were the bride and bridegroom and their friends. On the board before us were placed three plates (a very unusual thing in St Kilda), one filled with mutton, one filled with barley bannocks, and the third filled with cheese. The rest had their mutton and bread in wooden dishes made by nailing small boards together. There was neither soup nor drink of any kind on the board, nor used at any of their feasts. After a blessing was pronounced, no conversation for a while interrupted their eating, but afterwards there was some general conversation. When we came out, the women and boys were lounging about the house; the former waiting to get a piece of bread and mutton as a reward for their baking and grinding. Their portion being given out to them, the boys were seated at the table to consume what remained; when these were removed, all went home.'

Most marriages on the island involved partners who were already related to one another, but if some small and isolated communities have suffered from the ill-effects of intermarriage, St Kilda was not one of them. The common but unscientific assumption that consanguinity automatically leads to madness, deformity and a general debility among populations as well as individuals, is not supported by the example of St Kilda. The islanders had always intermarried, and although fresh blood was occasionally introduced when the men went on wife-hunting expeditions to other parts of the Hebrides and by immigration, consanguineous marriages were the rule rather than the exception.

Incest taboos were nonetheless enforced and the St Kildans took great care to examine the degrees of consanguinity in any proposed union. When the population of the island was up around the 200 mark the danger of marrying too close was slight, but even in the late history of the island, when the community was much reduced in number and generally on the decline, near marriages were rare. A survey taken in the 1860s showed that among the fourteen married couples on the island there was not one case of first cousins marrying, and only five where the couples were second cousins. These five had produced between them seventeen surviving children, none of whom were defective in either body or mind. But from the end of the 19th century until the evacuation in 1930 the health of the community, for a number of reasons, steadily declined; the islanders had become prone to every kind of illness, and inbreeding may well have aggravated a situation which was already serious.

The part played by immigration in maintaining both the health and the numbers of St Kilda's population is not easy to assess due to the lack of records. After the early settlements of the island there was probably a slow trickle of immigrants, who came over from the Hebrides or were delivered up by shipwrecks on the shores of Hirta. They may not have always been welcomed by the St Kildans, but on at least one occasion, when the island had to be almost entirely repopulated from outside, the community owed its continued existence to immigration.

In 1723 an old man from St Kilda went on a visit to Harris,

caught smallpox and died there. The following year some of his relatives went over to the Long Island to bring back his belongings. Among them were the old man's clothes, which, it seems, were still infectious. Certainly when the party of mourners returned to St Kilda with the clothes almost everyone on the island came down with smallpox. Because of the islanders' total lack of immunity the effects of the disease were devastating; most of them died. Some of the men, however, had gone on a fowling expedition to Boreray before the epidemic struck, and because there were not enough able bodied men on Hirta to fetch them back in the boat, they stayed there and escaped infection, somehow managing to survive until the next visit from the steward. When they returned to the main island they found only four adults and twenty-six children still alive, most of the houses deserted, the crops gone to seed and the cattle running wild. Death had followed upon death until the survivors were too few and too weak even to bury the corpses.

The community had to begin life again with less than forty people, many of them still too young to be of service; but there is evidence that help came in the form of immigration from other islands. In the Minutes of the Directors of the Society for the Propagation of Christian Knowledge for 1731 there is a reference to 'Hirta, which Island by the yearly transporting of people to it will soon be populous again'. Despite the enormity of the loss it had sustained St Kilda recovered well and quickly. Life continued much as it had done before the epidemic and by 1799 the population of the island had reached one hundred.

It is possible that at a much earlier date the population of St Kilda may have been similarly decimated, but by treachery rather than disease. One of the oldest stories connected with St Kilda tells of two brothers, Duncan and Farquar Mor, who were renowned sheep-stealers from the Isle of Lewis. They were feared throughout the Hebrides for their great strength and courage, which carried them to all the islands, even as far as the Flannans, in search of sheep and other plunder. One time they came to St Kilda with the intention of robbing the islanders. For several days they enjoyed the hospitality of the St Kildans and relaxed in the comfort of their homes; but on the evening of the fifth day, Duncan, who had climbed up to the top of Oiseval, suddenly started crying out that he could see warships in the sound of Boreray. The terrified natives needed little persuading by Farquar that the only thing to do was to hide in the temple and take sanctuary by the

horns of the altar. The moment the gullible St Kildans were all
safely inside the church the two sheep thieves blocked the entrance and laid whatever word and grass they could find against
the outside walls. Setting a precedent perhaps for what was to
become standard practice in Scottish history, Duncan and Farquar
proceeded to set fire to the church and roast its occupants alive.

In this way they accounted for everyone on the island—except
one old woman, who had been over at Gleann Mor and had not
heard Duncan's warning. On her way back to the village she
detected a strange smell (not unlike the smell of burning flesh),
which she accurately judged to be a sign that all was not well. Instead of investigating further she had the sense to hide herself
in a cave somewhere on the south side of Village Bay. When
darkness came she crept down into the empty village and discovered the brothers' crime. While the two murderers slept she took
what food she could find and returned to her cave. For several
months the old woman managed to survive, hiding by day and
stealing food by night, without being found out.

One day the steward's boat appeared on the horizon for the
annual visit to collect the rent. Duncan and Farquar went down
to the shore to meet him, confident that their uncandid version
of what had happened to the islanders would be accepted without question. But the old woman who had been watching and
waiting for this moment, came down from her hiding place on
the hill and told the steward the true story. The steward believed
her version and at once ordered Duncan and Farquar to be seized.
They were taken and marooned on Soay, where it was thought
they would not survive long without fire. But as the steward and
his men were leaving they overheard Duncan asking Farquar if
he had got the flint and tinder safe. Having attended to this detail
the steward decided to leave Duncan on Soay and move his
brother to Stac an Armin, but Farquar refused to stay and swam
after the boat pleading for mercy until he drowned.

On Soay Duncan managed to live a little longer. He built a
wall to protect himself from the north wind and lived in a cave
which still bears his name. The Little Old Woman of the Red
Fell, as she came to be known, left St Kilda with the steward and
for a time the island was deserted. She returned again, however,
a few years later to provide a new community with a transient
link with those who had been there before.

CHAPTER FOUR

Death, Legends and Beliefs

'The Celt is the most melancholy of men. He has turned everything to superstitious uses, and every object of nature, even
the unreasoning dreams of sleep, are mirrors which flash back
death upon him. . . . In his usual avocations death is ever near
him and that consciousness turns everything to omen.'

ALEXANDER SMITH

Deserted cemeteries often enjoy a longer half-life than the ruins of
places where people have lived. The graveyard on Hirta still bears
poignant witness to the departed community's lonely struggle for
existence. Immured in a sad oval of stone, Cill-Chriosd, the
Sepulchre of Christ, looks out across the roofless houses of the village to the bay beyond. An empty post and a red hinge are all
that remain of the wooden gate which once kept out the islanders'
cattle and sheep; lichen encrusts the random gravestones that
emerge at unexpected angles from the overgrowth of rank vegetation; iris flags take light and shade from the wind as they
bend where it blows. Despite the years of neglect and decay it is
the only place on the island where the past keeps constant vigil
over the present.

When there was a death in St Kilda the news was cried
throughout the island so that everyone could stop work and return home. The relatives of the deceased at once began to howl
and wail and to watch over the body for the next two or three
days or as long as it was kept inside the house. Dirges were sung
and laments composed, telling of the good deeds and fine character of the dead man, commending his soul. While the women
watched and sang and wept, the men set about making a coffin
with whatever wood was available. Others were kept busy catching sheep belonging to the dead man's family and baking bread.
The amount of food prepared for the wake was proportionate to
the honour to be paid to the deceased. It was an expensive custom
for anyone who was unlucky enough to lose several relatives.

When the grave had been dug and everything was ready, the funeral cortège set out for Cill-Chriosd. The coffin was carried on two poles by four young men who led the procession in the course of the sun's shadow, even if this meant trampling down crops, from the house to the graveyard. When they arrived at the cemetery they waited for the shadow of the sun to reach a certain position—adults were buried in the afternoon, children in the evening. Some prayers were said as the grave was filled in; then the mourners sat down on the grass and stones to eat their bread and mutton.

After the funeral the island went into mourning for a week, during which time little or no work could be done, the people being so overcome with grief and emotion. A death in St Kilda affected the whole community very deeply; everyone knew or was related to the dead person; and in a small isolated society every man, woman and child played an important part in the fight for survival. The loss of any human life was a victory for the other side and a harsh reminder to the community of its frailty.

In common with other Celtic peoples the St Kildans retained close contact with the spirits of the dead. The departed were never allowed to depart altogether, only to change residence. Souls inhabited rocks, streams, flowers, birds, animals, the bottom of a well, the edge of a cliff, almost anywhere, doing penance until released by prayer.

These transmigrations inevitably inclined the islanders to be superstitious. If one believed that every natural object harboured a soul in torment it was difficult to be otherwise. But their beliefs and superstitions were founded in the reality of a practical relationship with nature, in the islanders' everyday dependence on its bounty and their perpetual fear of its vengeance.

The St Kildans observed natural signs. They told the time of day from the course of the sun, not through the sky but over the land, noting when it struck certain rocks and parts of the hills. When there was no sun they watched the tides. They made weather forecasts, based on careful observation of sea, sky and the behaviour of the birds. But their applied study of nature was pervaded by superstition and the elaborate signs for telling some fantasy in the future were as meaningful to them as the more mundane indications of an approaching storm.

Most superstitious beliefs in St Kilda were also to be found with slight variations in other islands of the Hebrides. At one time it was a common belief in the Western Isles that birds always came and hovered around the houses of powerful families when one of them was about to die. At the moment of death the mysterious bird disappeared. If the bird was white it meant that the spirit of the deceased would have no difficulty in attaining heaven. For poorer families the birds would not come so close but stayed in the fields or near the cemetery and screamed all night long. A version of this superstition existed in St Kilda, where it was believed that the sighting or hearing of a cuckoo signified the death of MacLeod or his steward. It could also mean that an extraordinary event had or was about to take place, or that a stranger was coming to the island, which gave it a fair chance of being proved right.

Many of the common presages of death, known throughout the Celtic West, were also believed by the St Kildans. The cry of the banshee signified death for all who heard it, the Will-o'-the-wisp for all who saw it. Lights were sometimes to be seen moving slowly between the cemetery and the house where a doomed person lay. The ninth wave called anyone to their death who listened to its reverberations, first placing its victims, whether animals or men, under a spell known as the Celtic Gloom. A woman washing shrouds at a well or a stream was also seen before death.

As might have been expected birds were the most popular mediums in St Kilda, though outsiders were not always convinced by their prophetic powers. 'On the unmeaning actions or idleness of such silly birds,' wrote Macaulay, 'on their silence, singing, chirping, chattering and croaking, on their feeding or abstinence, on their flying to the right hand or left, was founded an art.' The fulmar arrived in November and, despite its popularity with the islanders, was always considered a harbinger of bad news, probably because it usually came with the bad weather. If a heron came to the island it was thought to mean a visit by a witch from Lewis. Great Auks were also taken for witches.

One of the strangest bird phenomena was the 'Sluagh' or Spirit Host. This mysterious apparition most often accompanied a west wind (it never came from the east) consisting of a great multitude of spirits moving through the air in crescent formation like a flight of grey geese. The 'Sluagh' could pick a man up and transport him over long distances. Sometimes it would rescue a fowler who was in danger of falling at the cliff-face, but more often it would drop him to his death.

Many of the islanders' superstitions and primitive religious beliefs were attached to significant natural objects such as streams and stones. Water in St Kilda, always plentiful and delicious to drink, was highly esteemed by the natives and most wells or springs had some magical association or other. The water from the Well of Virtue (Tobar nam Buaidh), situated at the foot of Gleann Mor, was considered to have healing power over all illness and ailments. The well had its own god, to whom an altar had been built close by; and anyone who came to drink there had to bring him a small offering, usually shells, pebbles or pieces of cloth. If any of the islanders were about to set out on a sea voyage and the wind happened to be unfavourable, they would pay a visit to the Well of St Brendan (Tobar na Cille) on Ruaival. As soon as each man had stood over the well for a few seconds the wind would change and begin to blow in the right direction.

Another well with miraculous attributes was once found somewhere on the slopes of Conachair by an old St Kildan, who was walking back to the village carrying a dead sheep, when he noticed water bubbling out of the ground. He kneeled down to drink some and immediately regained his lost youth. Since he had never seen a well in this place before and was happily surprised by its powers of rejuvenation, he laid the sheep's carcass down on the ground to mark the spot and ran back to the village to tell the others. When they returned they could find neither the sheep nor the well. According to those who know about such things, if the man had left a piece of iron, however small, instead of the sheep, the well would not have disappeared.

Some of the stones, believed by the St Kildans to have magical powers, may have been disused altars from pre-Christian times. Often the original purpose of the altar and the name of its deity had been forgotten. The Stone of Knowledge (Clach an Eolas) supposedly gave the power of second sight to anyone who stood on it during the first day of the moon's quarter, and enabled them to foresee all the events affecting the island for the whole of that quarter. The Milking Stone, however, continued to be used as a sacrificial altar until the 19th century and retained its god, a benevolent deity known as Gruagach. She was thought to have been a woman of good family from the Scottish mainland who had become enchanted. The Milking Stone had an indentation into which the St Kildans poured libations of milk every Sunday to ensure that their cattle stayed fertile, produced good milk and were kept from harm.

The Stone of Virtues (Clach dotaig) was not an altar but a small, semi-transparent pebble which was highly prized both in St

Kilda and other parts of the West. To obtain it a raven's egg had to be stolen, boiled until hard, then returned to the nest. The raven would try to hatch the egg but after a while give up and fly away. With luck it would return carrying the Stone of Virtues in its beak.

Stories of fairies and instances of second sight were at one time common in St Kilda, but unfortunately, since the tradition of the islanders was oral, few survived the iron ruling of the 19th century missionaries, which strictly forbade all such frivolities. What stories do exist differ in no way from those found on other islands and parts of the mainland. The following story is told by the poetess, Euphemia MacCrimmon, who in 1862 (when the following recording was made) was the oldest living St Kildan.

'Donald (MacDonald) and another man, named John MacQueen, were going to Oiseval, the most eastern hill, to hunt sheep. As they were passing a little green hillock they heard churning in the hill. John MacQueen cried, "Ho! wife, give me a drink." A woman in a green robe came out and offered him a drink (of milk); but although he had asked for it, he would not take it. She then offered it to Donald, and he said he would take it with God's blessing, and drank it off. They then went to their hunting, when John MacQueen fell over a precipice and was killed; and it was thought he met his fate for having refused the drink.'

Another story tells of a woman, whose son had drunk the milk of a cow which had eaten the mothan. The mothan is a rare plant (perhaps the sandwort or the bog violet), only found on the tops of hills or cliffs in places inaccessible to animals. It was believed that whoever carried the mothan or ate it or drank it in milk would come to no harm. The woman was lying in bed one night, when she received a visit from two fairy women dressed in green who put a spell on her so that she could not speak. But to her son, who lay in a cot by her side, the fairies gave the gift of the tongue and he grew up to be a great talker, which was no mean asset in St Kilda.

Once a woman was away gathering peats at the north end of the island when she saw a small door open in a mound. Taking care to stick an iron knife into the earth for her own protection, she looked in and witnessed a tiny speckled cow give birth to a speckled calf with no ears. The woman recognized the sign of the malevolent water bull spirit and ran away in terror.

One day about thirty St Kildans went over to Soay on a fowling expedition. They had only just arrived on the island when they noticed a body floating face down in the sea below them. The dead man was wearing a shirt, a plaid and a grey coat; and on his back stood a seagull pecking at his neck. After about a quarter of an hour the corpse and its gruesome passenger suddenly disappeared. Not long after one of the men who had seen this strange apparition happened to slip and fall into the sea. He drowned and was seen again floating face down in the water in exactly the same place and dressed in exactly the same way as the man in the vision, with a seagull standing on his back eating the flesh of his neck.

Giants and men of great strength feature prominently in St Kildan lore. Callum Mor (Big Malcolm) built the beehive house named after him, which is situated behind the village near Tobar Childa, in the space of a single day. Although he was too lame to be a fowler Callum was enormously strong and managed to lift the huge blocks of stone, some of them weighing three-quarters of a ton or more, without any assistance. He built the home as a service for a friend, who had done him a good turn.

On Ruaival there is a large slab of stone which bridges a chasm in the rock. It is said to be the petrified form of a girl who fell while running away from a giant. She had seen the monster striding over the water from Soay and had started to run, but tripped and fell across the chasm. For her own safety she was turned into stone. Up on the Carn Mor there is a great scar in a rock where the giant left the imprint of his foot on his way over from Soay.

Inventing giants and attributing ancestors with exaggerated strength and other remarkable qualities is a common practice in many primitive societies. Among the St Kildans it was concomitant with a belief in their own relative inferiority. When Martin visited the island the natives took gloomy delight in showing him impossibly large stones which they claimed their fathers had been able to lift quite easily, but which they themselves could not even move. 'The present generation comes short of the last in strength and longevity,' wrote Martin, 'not withstanding this, any one inhabiting St Kilda, is always reputed stronger than two of the inhabitants belonging to the Isle of Harries, or the adjacent isles.'

Although they did not worship their ancestors, the St Kildans held them in great respect. The legendary strength of their fore-bears and their skill as fowlers and cragsmen served as an incentive for the living, even if the mythical standards, which they were supposed to have set were far too high to be kept up. Failure to climb a difficult stac or perform some other extraordinary feat was on the one hand regarded as a slur on the memory of those who had done it before, but on the other was accepted as necessary proof of their ancestors' superiority. The beauty of this outlook was that it induced effort and welcomed success, but at the same time, without encouraging failure, made it honourable. The system, however, only worked if the superiority of their ancestors was imaginary and standards basically remained the same. When the community went into a decline and the St Kildans lost all incentive to keep up with their ancestors, whose superiority soon became all too real, the deterministic character of the islanders, where it recognized failure, came to regard it as inevitable.

The combination of superstition and fatalism made the St Kildans extremely susceptible to religious influence. Although the unwritten constitution of the commonwealth allowed no man to have political power over others, it did not forbid religious leaders. When missionaries came to St Kilda in the 18th and 19th centuries many of them were able to set themselves up without opposition as spiritual dictators over the hearts and minds of the people. The hegemony of the missionaries played a considerable part in the downfall of the community, but the St Kildans themselves were partly to blame for allowing themselves to be so easily led. Their isolation and ignorance of the world made them vulnerable to most outside influence, but in matters of the spirit they left themselves wide open to all comers. The curious story of Roderick the Impostor, who, as a native of St Kilda, became the island's only indigenous spiritual leader (of consequence) on record, helps to make the easy ascendency of the missionaries over the natives in later history more intelligible. As told by both Martin and Macaulay the story has a definite bias and not a little irony, since both men were interested in replacing the tyranny of the Impostor with a brand of despotism which turned out to be worse by far.

When Martin arrived in St Kilda in June of 1697, Roderick the Great had been holding sway over the islanders for more than six years. He was twenty-four years of age, red-haired, large-boned and exceptionally strong. His prowess at climbing and fowling was already legendary. Like everyone else in St Kilda Roderick was illiterate, but he did not share the innocence of his fellow islanders. Macaulay described him as though he were preparing a pantomime-audience for the entrance of the demon king: 'The impostor was a native of Hirta and though born in this land of darkness and simplicity, had a vast share of sagacity and cunning. AMBITION was his leading principle, and LUST his secondary passion,

AVARICE was another strong ingredient in the composition of his mind.'

When he was eighteen years old, Roderick, who had never travelled to any of the other islands, let alone the mainland of Scotland, claimed that on his return from fishing one day he met a man in Lowland dress, wearing a hat and a cloak, who said he was John the Baptist. This man offered to give Roderick religious instruction so that he in turn might spread the Word to his countrymen. The Impostor told people about his vision and seeing that they were impressed informed them that John the Baptist had taken to visiting him every day. Gradually he established himself as a religious teacher and gained a hold over the St Kildans. He used the sacrament of confession as a device to penetrate the secrets of every household on the island and became a powerful man. Not neglecting his duty, he held frequent prayer meetings, at which he would preach eloquently and sing long rhyming psalms of his own composition to the enraptured islanders—for among other things the Impostor was a poet.

He imposed a new code of law on the community, forbidding the use of the Lord's Prayer, the Creed and the Ten Commandments, and replaced them with other versions of the same, which, he claimed, had been transmitted to him by John the Baptist. Although the Impostor only spoke Gaelic his new prayers were full of strange sounding words, many of them unknown in that part of the world, which naturally convinced the St Kildans of their authenticity. He introduced strict fasting on Fridays and a new way of killing sheep without using a knife. He also maintained that a certain piece of land, which he christened John's Hillock, had been consecrated by the Baptist and was therefore holy ground. On it there grew a bush which was equally sacred. If any cow or sheep happened to tread on the hallowed spot or touch the bush it had to be slain at once and eaten by Roderick and its owner. One reform, however, which the St Kildans resisted, was the Impostor's attempt to induce them to change their ancient burial custom by facing the heads of the dead to the south instead of to the east. Roderick suggested that if this was done they would immediately be carried up to heaven riding upon white horses, but the islanders stood their ground.

The Impostor used his position of authority to seduce as many of the women on the island as he possibly could. He composed a special hymn for women only, which, he said would preserve them from death in childbirth. Any woman who wanted to learn the hymn had to pay Roderick one sheep for the privilege. The hymn, of course, could only be taught in private, which gave him all the opportunities he needed. If a woman refused him, she was made to do penance by standing naked under a dammed-up waterfall, which was suddenly released upon her head. In winter this could become quite a trial and there were few who did not succumb in the end. One woman, however, who happened to be the officer's wife, managed to withstand Roderick's attempts to seduce her and even had the courage to tell her husband of his evil intentions. The officer, with a natural instinct for theatre, decided to hide himself behind the partition wall of his home during one of the hymn lessons—'There he stays until this lecher began to caress his wife, and then he thought himself obliged seasonably to appear for her rescue, and boldly reproved the impostor for his wicked practices.' But the officer did not expose the Impostor, who managed to patch things up between them to the extent that the two men became blood brothers and so entered into a pact of everlasting friendship. Since it was considered a very serious crime to break the bonds of blood brotherhood Roderick was able to continue his malpractices as if nothing had happened.

Eventually the St Kildans wearied of their religious leader. A small incident had given the lie to his infallibility. A cousin of the Impostor's called Muldonich, or Lewis, owned a ewe which had given birth to three lambs. One day they were seen feeding on the sacred bush on John's Hillock. Roderick immediately flew into a rage and ordered the lambs to be killed, but Muldonich refused. When he was not struck down dead as Roderick had warned, the people lost faith in him and by the time of Martin's visit they had become totally disenchanted. They asked the steward to take Roderick off the island. First they tried to flatter him into leaving by saying that MacLeod of Dunvegan was very much interested in meeting him, but Roderick saw through the ruse. In the end he had to be removed by force. The islanders, however, were afraid for Martin and his company, because Roderick, who was some-thing of a witch, supposedly could not put to sea without a storm getting up, but the party arrived in Harris without incident. Later the Impostor was taken to Dunvegan Castle where he confessed to his crimes and recanted before the presbytery. As a punishment he was made to wander on foot through the island of Skye from parish to parish making public confessions of his sins.

Ten years after Roderick's deposition the first missionary was sent to St Kilda, and during the next century a kind of orthodoxy was gradually established on the island, though it did not gain a stranglehold on the life of the community until the 19th century. Before 1800 the religion of the islanders was, as it had been since the time of the Culdees, a mixture of early Christianity and Druidism. Over the centuries there were occasional visits from wandering priests and MacLeod's chaplain from Dunvegan but their influence was slight. Until the arrival of the missionaries the St Kildans had their own priests, though little is known about them or their duties, other than that they were not men of great learning, nor much revered by their fellow islanders.

A reiver, called Coll MacDonald, who was the father of Montrose's famous lieutenant, Colkitto, raided St Kilda in 1615 and stole all the available food on the island killing cattle, horses and sheep and sparing only the lives of the inhabitants. Twenty-six years later the same man, who had 'made himself obnoxious to the law' in another context, turned up again in St Kilda. He had been beaten in battle, lost both his army and his right hand and was on the run. By coincidence he had jumped a boat which happened to be bound for St Kilda. On his arrival there the inhabitants immediately took to the caves thinking that they were all about to be killed. But Coll managed to persuade them that his intentions were friendly or at least that he was not in a fit state to do them any harm. As a gesture he handed round some snuff and showed them the stump at the end of his right arm. The St Kildans, who seemed to have forgiven the raid of 1615, took him in, and he lived with them for nearly a year. While he was on the island left-handed Coll fell out with the priest, a native of St Kilda, who only had a few very vague ideas about religion. When one day Coll began beating up the priest with his good arm, the islanders, who were generally dissatisfied with their holy man's performance, did nothing to stop him. They asked Coll if he thought that they should get rid of a man who called himself a priest but did not even know the Pater Noster or the Creed. Coll wisely answered that ignorance was no reason for deposing a priest and made amends for his past crimes by teaching the priest and his parishioners the Decalogue, the Creed and the Lord's Prayer.

The St Kildans did not really need spiritual directors. They were always a naturally religious people and saw to their own devotion. The kind of life they led in their wild and lonely world, with an unbroken circle of sea and sky for an horizon and little knowledge of what lay beyond, would have been impossible without religion. The dangers they faced everyday, their proximity to death and the elemental forces of nature, their unending struggle to survive made some kind of faith a necessity. At a primitive level it grew up from a respect for nature and became sublimated in the belief that the natural world was inhabited by spirits. Christianity without dispelling this notion had introduced ideas which reached beyond it and affected the way in which the people organized their lives. They related the social order of the island to the ritual and meaning of the new religion and vice versa; and with the help of such practical considerations as the small size and homeliness of the churches and the natural fellowship of the congregation successfully introduced a simple type of worship where communion really did mean sharing.

Perhaps the symbiosis of church and state was most evident in the celebration of religious feasts. The islanders observed at least seven holy days each year in honour of St Columba, St Brendan, Michaelmas, All Saints, Easter, Christmas and the New Year. The denominator common to all these feasts was the emphasis on sharing. No work was allowed, though the cows had to be milked and all the milk divided up among the people in the manner of the ancient love-feasts practised by the Early Christian monks. Christmas and New Year's Day were particularly happy occasions on which the whole island gave itself over to having a good time. The best of food and drink was prepared, sheep were slaughtered, bread was baked. Dancing and singing went on all day and night. For Michaelmas the St Kildans baked an enormous cake in honour of the archangel. Everyone on the island received a piece of this cake, which, they believed, afforded them Michael's friendship and protection. Later in the day there were horse races, in which the most skilful riders rode without saddles or bridles for no greater prize than the honour and glory which was bestowed upon the winner. On All Saints' day the men rode in a cavalcade from the beach up to the village taking it in turns to mount the horses, since there were not enough to go round.

Feasts were important to the islanders because of their particular religious and social significance; but they were also a testimony to the success of the community. They gave the opportunity for a kind of extravagance, a wild and short-lived exuberance, which the rest of the year was foreign to the St Kildan way of life. For a day and perhaps a night the ideality of existence on Hirta might almost be realized. And this provided an incentive to go on living there.

CHAPTER FIVE

A Simple Life

'But he shaved with a shell when he chose.
'Twas the manner of Primitive Man.'

ANDREW LANG

St Kilda man was never a sub-species of homo sapiens, but he did develop, in the same way as the island's true sub-species of mice and wren, certain peculiar physical characteristics due to the influence of the environment. Centuries of scaling the cliffs after sea-birds had made him unusually strong and agile, and because the St Kildan fowler, like the wren, had learnt to grip the rock with his bare feet, his toes had acquired almost prehensile capacity and were set wider apart than on a normal foot. The instep too was thicker and the ankle more muscular with a heavier bone structure better suited to climbing. The women, who even in St Kilda might have regarded such advantages as afflictions, were happily for them unaffected.

In all other respects the physical make-up and appearance of the islanders were quite ordinary, though descriptions vary from century to century. Martin observed that 'both sexes are naturally very grave, of a fair complection' and suggested that any dark-haired St Kildans had probably come to the island quite recently. He drew attention to the lightness of the men's beards, who managed to grow 'but a few hairs upon the upper lip and point of the chin', and these not before the age of thirty or thirty-five. The Norse influence was also suggested by their long, aquiline faces and the contemplative cast of their features. Although the type was common enough throughout the Hebrides the blood of the Vikings may have been less diluted in St Kilda than on the other islands.

The early authors mostly agreed on the beauty of the St Kildans, especially of the women, though the men were sometimes criticized for being short, thick-set and rather awkward looking. The average height of the men in the 1870s was 5 feet 6 inches and in Martin's time it was probably little different. But in other respects the physical appearance of the 19th century St Kildans seems to have undergone a change for the worse, or perhaps it had something to do with the attitudes of those who described them. Certainly immigration had affected the stock and as the community declined the health of the people suffered, but as early as the 1830s the Reverend Neil Mackenzie held the opinion that 'as a race the natives now are undersized and far from being robust or healthy'. A later observer complained that the women were stout and squat and that both sexes emitted an unpleasant odour, which he attributed to the large quantities of oleaginous sea-birds consumed by the islanders. Not all later descriptions were derogatory. Most pointed out that the islanders looked well-fed and some praised their bright eyes, small white teeth and intelligent, even noble, expressions. No doubt there was an element of finding what you look for on both sides.

Old photographs show that in one respect the appearance of the men had changed radically since the 17th century. Somewhere along the way they had learnt how to grow marvellous flourishing beards, which give what may be a false impression of both wisdom and ease. But there can be little ambiguity about the faces of the women. They bear clearly the marks of strain from what had become an unrelentingly severe life. It is difficult to believe that Macaulay could have written in 1758: 'the women here are mostly handsome, and their complexion fresh and lively, as their features are regular and fine. . . . There are some of them, who if properly dressed, and genteely educated, would, in my opinion, be reckoned extraordinary beauties in the gay world.'

To those unfamiliar with the traditional female role in the highlands and islands of Scotland the St Kildan women would appear to have been treated little better than beasts of burden, for they did nearly all the work on the island which involved carrying. Water, milk, birds, peat, stores, anything that they could lift was automatically their charge. 'It was no uncommon thing to see the young men helping to rope the bags of meal and flour which had come by steamer on to the women's backs. Sheep, coal, or any burden was carried from the pier by the women as a rule—very occasionally the men,' wrote a lady visitor in 1909. Things had been better in former days when there were horses on the island but even then the women had to work hard. In summer, morning and evening, they climbed over the hill to milk the cows and ewes in Gleann Mor carrying bundles of grass for the cows on the way out and milk pails on the way home. Their other activities, apart from ordinary household duties, included grinding corn, spinning, digging in the fields, making cheese, puffin snaring and plucking and salting down the bird catches. When the boat went out they were expected to help carry it up and down the beach.

Although their work did not give the women equal status with the men, at least not by 20th century standards, it made them very like the men in their ways. They had their own informal assembly which met, usually over the spinning, to discuss their affairs and to sing and make up songs. They also had a queen, who was chosen from among the unmarried women of the island, originally as a leader of the women's puffin snaring expeditions to Boreray in the summer. In the 1830s the islanders elected a girl from the mainland called Betty Scott as honorary Queen of St Kilda, because in their eyes she was more beautiful, accomplished and better educated than any of their own women. When Betty Scott, who was housekeeper to the minister, Neil Mackenzie, was drowned in a boating accident, the title of queen passed first to her daughter and from then on to the most beautiful woman on the island. This tradition and the story of the Amazon, as well as certain anomalies in the division of labour between the sexes, have led to speculation that St Kilda may at one time have been a matriarchal society, but as long as the vital work of fowling, upon which the survival of the community depended, was carried out by the men, it seems an unlikely hypothesis.

Not long before Martin visited St Kilda the islanders used to dress entirely in sheepskins, but by the end of the 17th century they had mostly adopted a more modern form of dress. Lambskin hats, however, along the lines of the Russian astrakhan, survived into the 19th century. In summer when they were out working on the hill or the cliffs, both men and women wore no clothes other than a woollen shirt. Over these woollen shirts, which served as undergarments in winter, the men wore a short doublet, which in turn was covered by a voluminous plaid reaching down to the knees and cinched at the waist by a leather belt. The two ends of the plaid were secured by a pin, usually made from a fulmar bone or the beak of an oyster catcher. This was the nearest the St Kildans ever came to wearing kilts. Breeches, wide and open at the knee, had already made an appearance by 1697 and from then onwards the St Kildans wore what was basically traditional Lowland dress. In the 19th century the men wore trousers and waistcoats over their woollen shirts and wound a thick scarf about their necks, reserving their jackets for Sunday.

Men and women's clothing alike was tailored and sewn by the

men, who also weaved the thick cloth, known as blue kelt (though it was sometimes brown with a stripe) from which most of the garments were made. The costume of the women did not vary much down the centuries. Over a roughly-made dress of blue kelt they wore a plaid gathered at the breast with a buckle, fashioned out of a penny beaten thin, a bent nail or even a fish-hook. All the women wore headdresses of linen, often a brilliant scarlet colour, with a plait of hair falling down each cheek and tied in a knot where it reached the breast. Married women were distinguished by a white frill which they carried like a comb in the front of their head-kerchief. In later years plaids in Rob Roy tartan imported from the mainland were considered very fine and worn on Sundays and special occasions with white muslin caps. When the women were working in the fields they used to gird up their skirts quite short with a sash around the waist, so that they could move more freely.

Until boots and stockings were introduced by tourists in the 19th century, two types of more primitive shoe were in use in St Kilda. The oldest of these was made out of the neck of a gannet. Cut close to the eyes and to the breast of the bird, the skin of the neck was reversed so that the down was on the inside. It was then sewn up at the longer breast end, which received the foot while the heel rested on the crown of the head. The shoe only lasted four or five days but it was light, comfortable and easily replaced. The 'brog tiondadh' or turned shoe was a type of brogue made out of sheep skin or cow hide tanned and softened with the root of tormentil. It was held in position by a leather thong and left open at the sides to let the water run out. But in the summer months both men and women would go barefoot. Children rarely, if ever, wore shoes.

St Kildan dress was rough, simple and designed for warmth and function rather than decoration. Basically it differed little from that worn in other parts of the Hebrides, but the St Kildans had no means of keeping pace with the fashions of the mainland, so that visitors to the islands were generally delighted by the antiquated and picturesque costumes of the natives. Inevitably the tourists gradually succeeded in spoiling their own pleasure. A visitor of 1900 complained of seeing a St Kildan woman wearing a Piccadilly fringe and her little boy sporting a Dicky bow-tie. Such incongruities did not become a primitive culture.

The most distinctive form of architecture in St Kilda is the cleit. These primitive storehouses date back in design to prehistoric times but they continued to be built and used by the islanders until 1930. In them they dried peat, nets, corn, and preserved birds, meat, fish and eggs. There are still more than a thousand of them dotted about all over the island, some built on flat ground others in the most precarious places, on the steepest hillside or half-way down a cliff. Their distribution at first seems to be totally haphazard but it probably depended on the availability of suitable stone. A cleit looks like a huge skep built of small flattish boulders which have been made to overlap until they meet to form a dome. The top of the cleit was capped with green turf to keep the rain out, while its walls were built with plenty of cavities to let the wind through. This was the beauty of its construction, that it made use of but at the same time defeated nature. It represented a small triumph of human ingenuity, and as such was the basic symbol of St Kildan life.

'The whole body of this little people live together, like the inhabitants of a town or city. All their houses are built in two rows, abundantly regular and facing one another, with a tolerable causeway in the middle, which they call the "Street".' The old village, as described by Macaulay in the 18th century, was situated in the most sheltered part of Village Bay; protected from the winds by the heavy shoulders of Conachair, it received a fair amount of sun and was well drained. The village consisted of between twenty-five and thirty dwellings of the black house type strung out along the half mile of street, which ran gradually up hill following the line of a natural embankment between the factor's house and Tobar Childa. Some of the houses were of an earlier beehive design, dating from the first centuries AD to the Middle Ages. Like cleits they were stone built without the use of wood, corbelled and roofed with turf rather than thatch, which meant that they were in no way dependent on an agricultural economy. But they differed from cleits in that beehive walls were constructed to keep out the wind (with the help of turf packed into any crevices), not let it in. They were low-doored and strongly built, with small circular chambers off the main walls, reached only from the inside and probably used as dormitories or storage rooms. When they were in use, the beehive houses would have been entirely covered in turf and almost indistinguishable from green hillocks.

By 1697, however, the islanders were mostly living in black houses of the type found throughout the Hebrides at that time. They were built with immensely thick double walls which were filled with a mixture of gravel and peat for insulation. The roof, a wooden frame covered with thatch, reached only to the inner wall, leaving no eaves to be caught by the wind and draining its water into the cavity between the walls. The peat and gravel filtered the water through to the ground. It never penetrated the interior of the house because the stones of the inner wall were bedded with an outwards slope, but it kept the cavity material moist and therefore more windproof. The roof was held in place by stone weights and ropes made of straw or twisted heather and secured by gannet's beaks. A small hole was left in one corner between the roof and the walls to allow some light to penetrate and at the same time provide a chimney for the smoke from the peat fire, which was kept in night and day on a circular hearth in the middle of the floor. The entrance, more like a tunnel than a door due to the thickness of the walls, also served as a vent and a window; but neither opening did much good, and it is to its dark, soot-blackened, smoky interior that the black house owes its name.

The inside of the house was divided into two rooms by a movable stone partition called a 'fallan'. In winter and spring one side was occupied by the family, the other by the cow. The byre end of the house faced towards the Bay so that the drain could carry manure directly on to the cultivation strips; it also acted as a buffer between the cold winds and the living area. A bed recess or 'crub' roofed with a large stone slab was let into the back wall of the house, partly so as to have more space, but also to avoid sleeping on the floor where manure was collected. The principle probably evolved from the dormitory cells of the earlier beehive houses. Inside the 'crub', which resembled a baker's oven, the islanders slept on straw, even though St Kilda was famous for its feathers. Young and old of both sexes huddled together like puffins in a burrow, covering themselves with blankets and using rolled up clothing for pillows. Other furnishings were sparse, consisting of a few stools, a quern for grinding corn, a 'clach soluis' or stone lamp filled with fulmar oil with smouldering peat for a wick, a pitcher for water, a 'cragan' or clay cooking-pot and some low dishes for eating and drinking out of.

The streamlined shape of the black house gave it the awkward look of an up-turned boat, but it was nonetheless a successful design. Despite the horrified concern of early 19th-century visitors at the lack of hygiene, the islanders did not live 'in hovels like animals', as one of them put it, but in houses which were built to withstand the rigours of the climate. They stayed warm, dry and draught-free all the year round and consequently made healthy and comfortable homes.

There is little trace left now of those early black houses or of the village first described by Martin and Maculay. In 1836 the Reverend Neil MacKenzie persuaded the St Kildans to rebuild the entire settlement 200 yards further down the slopes of Conachair. The islanders appear to have used the stones from the old houses to put up the thirty new buildings, which were also of the black house type, though they had no 'crub' in the back wall and were improved by a tiny window and a wooden lock on the door. The latter was of ingenious though somewhat pointless native design. More sophisticated furnishings also reached the island about this time due to the influence of Mackenzie. Stone lamps and clay pots were replaced in iron; kettles, wooden dishes, chests, box-beds and chairs were all innovations. In most respects, however, the new village was much the same as the old and island life continued as before. The houses had been built facing the same direction, the fire remained in the middle of the floor and the sooty thatch was replaced every spring and used as manure. But less than thirty years later the village was to be rebuilt yet again, this time bringing unprecedented and drastic change to the community.

The black-house style of living was common to most of the Hebrides, but the St Kildan diet, on the other hand, was more distinctive. It was based on sea-birds: gannets, fulmar, puffins, guillemots and razorbills were consumed in large numbers by the islanders, who preferred them to any other food. The bird season opened in February with the welcome arrival of guillemots and razorbills; followed in March by the mature gannets; in summer by the fulmar and puffins, and in the autumn by the young gannets or 'gugas'. The birds were eaten either fresh when in season or cured. Salt was used as a preservative in later years but in the 17th century it was still considered a luxury in St Kilda, though as a surrogate the islanders used the ashes of seaware, picked when young so as not to give too strong a taste.

In 1696 the islanders consumed 22,600 gannets, which gave every man, woman and child 113 birds apiece, but this was considered a poor year. Gannets once plucked and cleaned were slit down the back, carefully rolled and preserved in piles, which were built up inside the cleits. As well as those intended for export, each family set several hundred 'gugas' aside for winter consumption. By the middle of the 18th century the gannet had been replaced by the fulmar as the staple food, probably as a result of fulmar oil and feathers becoming valuable exports, though there may have been other reasons.

Both gannnets and fulmar could be eaten either roast or boiled, but it was advisable to remove the backbone and first allow the carcass to soak in water before cooking, to get rid of the fishy taste. Gugas are covered in a thick layer of fat and have been known to throw the most determined gourmets, but the fulmar, reputedly, has a taste which is almost worth acquiring. According to John Ross, school teacher to St Kilda in 1889, 'The fulmar, when young and fresh is best roasted. Indeed, when properly done this way and when one has the nerve to start, it tastes fairly well. Something like young pork, but as tender as chicken.' Roast puffin also has a certain appeal; the carcass was split down the back and opened out flat like a kipper; it was then propped upright on the hearth and grilled in front of the fire. Puffins were usually eaten fresh or slightly smoked from being hung in the rafters.

The only condiment which the St Kildans took with their food was made from the oily fat of young gannets melted down and stored in the stomachs of the mature birds. They ate this 'giben', as it was called, with everything from fish to vegetables, pouring it cold on to hot food, like olive oil or butter. 'They boil the sea-plants, dulse, and slake, melting the giben upon them instead of butter, and upon the roots of silver-weed and dock·boiled, and also with their scurvy-grass stoved, which is very purgative,' wrote Martin, '. . . it is become the common vehicle that conveys all their food down their throats.' Eggs were another valuable by-product of seabirds and were consumed in vast quantities by the St Kildans. During Martin's visit the steward's party of sixty ailing men from Skye were given 16,000 eggs by the inhabitants, which turned out to be more than they could handle. Instead of regaining their strength they became sick and feverish and, to the amazement of the islanders, their veins swelled up. 'The eggs are found to be of an astringent and windy quality to strangers,' wrote Martin, wise after the event, 'but, it seems are not so to the inhabitants.' The St Kildans preserved their eggs, in cleits, burying them in peat ash to keep them dry, and leaving them anything up to eight months to improve the flavour. They sometimes took the eggs fresh from the nest and drank them off raw, but they liked them best of all when they had turned.

In the winter months mutton, either fresh or dried, and occassionally beef was eaten by the islanders, but for the rest of the year red meat was reserved for special occasions, such as weddings, funerals and feasts. Bread too was considered something of a luxury, particularly in the 19th century when cereal production on the island began to fall, though porridge continued to supply the farinaceous element in their diet. When there was a celebration it was always the responsibility of the men to see to the cooking of the meat, which they prepared in several different ways. A favourite recipe was to wrap the joint in the raw hide of the animal and bury it in the hot ashes of a large peat fire. The results could be delicious and the skilful cook would acquire a reputation for his art, which put him in high demand.

The St Kildans ate three times a day. Breakfast was taken at about nine o'clock and consisted of milk, eggs (if there were any), porridge and sometimes a puffin or fulmar, boiled in the porridge to give it flavour. For dinner, the main meal of the day, eaten at any time that was convenient, there was either roast sea-bird with sorrel or potatoes, mutton in winter or fish. If the men were going out on an expedition they took with them a simple picnic of oat-cakes, cheese and a drink of whey milk. The evening meal, like dinner, was a movable feast and might be taken as late as 10 or 11 pm, especially in winter when the islanders worked at weaving and spinning into the early hours of the morning. It normally con-sisted of eggs, porridge, fulmar and cheese. The St Kildans mostly drank water or milk, though at one time they made beer by blending the juice of nettle roots with barley, which gave off a kind of yeast and, according to Martin, produced 'good ale, so that when they drink plentifully of it, it disposes them to dance merrily'.

No attempt at growing vegetables on Hirta ever met with much success, due largely to the salt-laden atmosphere and the heavy showers of spray which dashed over the island in winter, but be-tween sad-looking cabbages and occasional turnips the islanders made do with the indigenous herbs and weeds of both land and sea. Potatoes were introduced in the 18th century, but though they grew quite well they were not popular with the St Kildans. Fruit was never a part of their diet and the first apple ever to be seen on the island was brought out by a visitor in the second half of the 19th century. It caused a great deal of astonishment.

If the diet of the St Kildans tended to be monotonous, it was largely due to their partiality for sea-birds. Fish, by comparison, was considered a very dull dish; not sufficiently oily, it was thought to have no 'substance'. Often they would throw the body of the fish to the dogs and keep only the liver for making stuffed fish-heads, a favourite delicacy known as 'ceann-cropic'. But towards the end of the 19th century their diet was to change and fish to become almost their staple food.

On the whole the people appear to have been extremely well fed throughout their history. A bad summer, nonetheless, affecting the harvest of birds or crops, could lead to severe hardships in the following spring. In July of 1841 the Reverend Neil Mackenzie made the following entry in his journal : 'The people are suffering very much from want of food. During spring, ere the birds came, they literally cleared the shore not only of shell-fish, but even of a species of sea-weed that grows abundantly on the rocks within the sea-mark. . . . Now the weather is coarse, birds cannot be found, at least in such abundance as their needs require.' Being accustomed to plenty, however, their needs were substantial, and as late as 1887 a man from the Isle of Skye, comparing the St Kildans to crofters in others parts of the Hebrides, observed, 'They are the best fed people in creation'.

When a primitive community is able to produce a surplus of food and has learnt how to store it, it begins to devote more energy to the development of skills and arts which are not necessarily har- nessed to the every day business of survival. In the case of St Kilda a food surplus was probably achieved from earliest times, but at least since the 14th century most of it went into paying the rent. Consequently life on the island never really got beyond the stage of being a struggle for existence, even if at times the existence was a comfortable one. What leisure the St Kildans did have they spent well, but with less thought for posterity than for enjoyment. On the whole island there is only one artefact which suggests a skill un- connected with staying alive. It is a simple relief of a Celtic cross carved on a stone, which was originally part of Christ church and later built into the front wall of one of the 1860 cottages.

As a form of relaxation the men used to play a kind of shinti on the beach with short clubs and balls made of wood. They played hard and loved winning; there were usually prizes of eggs, birds, fish-hooks or tobacco. Swimming and diving was another favourite sport in the summer. But in later years the islanders forgot how to swim and all sports and amusements were banned by the mission- aries.

The chief sport of the St Kildans, however, was less susceptible to the whims of the Church since it coincided with the inexpendable activity of fowling. Rock-climbing not only provided excitement but a reason to develop a useful skill beyond the limits of exped- iency. A wish to excel at the cliff-face was the cultural inheritance of every young St Kildan and encouraged personal competition, though as the male population decreased and the community

became demoralized fewer risks were taken and climbing lost some
of its kudos. But up until the evacuation the St Kildans would
occasionally put on displays of rock-climbing for visitors, if the
price was right. Letting out wild Gaelic cries they would bounce
down the face of the cliff hundreds of feet above the sea, sailing
through the air, swinging on the rope to get past an overhang,
singing and dancing all the while and giving an impression of grace-
ful ease and a freedom rediscovered.

'The power of music is felt everywhere,' wrote Macaulay in 1758.
'The St Kildans are enthusiastically fond of it, whether in the vocal
or instrumental way : The very lowest tinklings of the latter, throws
them into an extasy of joy. I have seen them dancing to a bad
violin much to my satisfaction : Even the old women in the isle act
their part in the great assemblies, and the most agile dancers are
here, as well as everywhere else, very great favourites. They delight
much in singing, and their voices are abundantly tuneful.' The
women used to sing constantly while they were working, 'and the
men, if pulling at the oar, exert all the strength of their skill in
animating the party, by chanting away some spirited song adapted to
the business in hand.' Music in St Kilda, as elsewhere in the
Hebrides, provided a form of relaxation which included rather than
excluded work. As with the sport of rock-climbing it helped make
what had to be done fun to do. Many of the St Kilda songs were
about everyday events and activities such as the making of cloth
or the milking of a cow, but not all were steadfastly 'adapted to the
business in hand' either rhythmically or by subject matter. Music
and poetry were easily the most developed, if not the only forms of
artistic expression enjoyed by the islanders. Their songs about love
and death, about the beauty and accomplishments of the women
or the heroism and strength of the men reflect in simple language
the essential precariousness of their lonely existence, but at the same
time they remind one that life in St Kilda, however limited by the
emptiness of its horizon, was as complete as it is anywhere else.

    The reputation, however, which Hirta once had for producing
great poetry is not altogether supported by the few bits and pieces
which have survived. There was a time when anyone who slept a
night on top of Conachair awoke a poet in the morning, and
Martin testifies that several islanders of both sexes had a genius for
poetry, but whether his critical sense was as well developed as his
powers of observation is not certain. But he was at least speaking

from experience, unlike Dr Johnson, who without having heard a word of St Kilda poetry was able to draw the conclusion:

'It must be very poor because they have very few images.'

'But there may be a poetical genius to combine these, and in short to make poetry of them,' replied Boswell, who liked the idea of St Kilda better than Johnson.

'But, Sir,' said Dr Johnson, 'a man cannot make fire but in proportion as he has wood. He cannot coin guineas but in proportion as he has gold.'

Whether Martin or Johnson was right made little difference to the St Kildans, who by the middle of the 19th century had almost entirely forgotten their musical heritage and lost whatever talent for poetry they once may have had. The reciting of poems, of old stories and traditions, the performing of dances and the playing of secular music was banned by the missionaries. Psalms and hymns could be sung in church only, but the islanders seemed to have little aptitude for religious music. Despite their enthusiasm — in church on Sundays everybody always sang their own versions of the tune as loud as they could without any attempt at harmony or co-ordination — the sound of their voices, once described as 'abundantly tuneful', soon came to be compared to the baying of a pack of hyenas.

The missionaries did their work well and very little remains of St Kilda music, either words or tunes. Some St Kilda songs, however, were collected by Alexander Carmichael in 1865. He heard them from the old poetess, Euphemia MacCrimmon, who by then was eighty-four and still remembered them from the old days. She was severely reprimanded by the minister for reciting the poems and songs, and Carmichael was told off for stirring her memory and encouraging her, but luckily both of them persevered. The following love song in the form of a conversation was written by Euphemia MacCrimmon's own mother and father before they were married.

St Kilda Lilt

He :   Away bent spade, away straight spade,
        Away each goat and sheep and lamb;
        Up my rope, up my snare—
        I have heard the gannet upon the sea!
        Thanks to the Being, the gannets are come,
        Yes, and the big birds along with them;
        Dark dusky maid, a cow in the fold!

A brown cow, a brown cow, a brown cow beloved,
A brown cow, my dear one, that would milk the milk for
thee,
Ho ro ru ra ree, playful maid,
Dark dusky maid, cow in the fold!
The birds are a-coming, I hear their tune!

She: Truly my sweetheart is the herdsman
Who would threaten the staff and would not strike!

He: Mary, my dear love is the maid,
Though dark her locks, her body is fragrant!

She: Thou art my handsome joy, thou art my sweetheart,
Thou gavest me the first honied fulmar!

He: Thou art my turtle-dove, thou art my mavis,
Thou art my melodious harp in the sweet morning.

She: Thou art my hero, thou art my basking sunfish,
Thou gavest me the puffin and the black-headed guillemot.

He: The mirth of my eyes and the essence of my joy thou art,
And my sweet—sounding lyre in the mountain of mist.

Many of the St Kilda songs were mournful laments in minor
keys. The music was wild and eerie and imitated the crying of sea-
birds and the singing of seals. The following song is written by an
island woman who lost all the men in her family at sea in a boating
tragedy.

It was no crew of landsmen
Crossed the ferry on Wednesday;
'Tis tidings of disaster if you live not.

What has kept you so long from me?
Are the high sea and the sudden wind catching you,
So that you could not at once give her sail?

'Tis a profitless journey
That took the noble men away,
To take our one son from me and from Donald.

My son and my three brothers are gone,
And the one son of my mother's sister,
And, sorest tale, that will come or has come, my husband.

What has set me to draw ashes
And to take a spell at digging
Is that the men are away with no word of their living.

I am left without fun or merriment
Sitting on the floor of the glen;
My eyes are wet, oft are tears on them.

CHAPTER SIX

An Arcadian in Glasgow

'But, oh, o'er all, forget not Kilda's race,
On whose bleak rocks, which brave the wasting tides,
Fair nature's daughter, virtue, yet abides.'

WILLIAM COLLINS

A consequence of St Kilda's remoteness was the obliviousness of its inhabitants to the affairs of the outside world. As far as they were concerned the world was their island—of what lay beyond, they had but the haziest concept. Time was measured by the seasons and history divided up into eras by the lives of the MacLeods and their stewards, who were remembered in accounts of their various deeds and misdeeds. To the St Kildans their chief was the embodiment of all power and wealth. Those who had been on a visit to Dunvegan reported back to the others what they had seen there. They were amazed by such things as windows, looking glasses and tapestries (which they considered vain and unnecessary), and by MacLeod's habit of riding everywhere on horseback. He owned what seemed to them like all the countries of the world and although they had heard about the king they found it difficult to believe that he could be superior. Historical events which did not concern St Kilda or MacLeod in some way, and there were not many that did, were of little interest to the islanders. In 1746 when General John Campbell arrived on Hirta with a detachment of troops looking for the fugitive Bonnie Prince Charlie, the St Kildans were able to say quite truthfully that they had never heard of him, though they did know that their chief had recently been at war with what was thought to be 'a great woman', and were under the impression that he had won. In 1815 the islanders were completely unaware of Napoleon or recent events in Europe, but were very much concerned whether the American War of Independence, which (having a limited concept of war) they assumed was still in progress, would put up the price of tobacco.

If St Kilda was both ignorant and innocent of the world, the world, though perhaps less innocent, was never very knowledgeable about St Kilda. Because it was so difficult to get to, and not always thought worth the trip, St Kilda tended to be neglected by events. In the late 15th century when James IV claimed the islands of Scotland for his own, he omitted Hirta ostensibly on the grounds that it was too far away for him to protect. But most likely he came to the same conclusion as MacLeod, that it was not worth taking fighting men from an island, whose inhabitants were harmless people quite unfitted for the battlefield. The same attitude prevailed in the 19th and 20th centuries, where the lack of exploitable resources in St Kilda, with the possible exception of tourism, largely accounted for the failure to set up adequate communications between the island and the mainland. Before the first official census was taken in 1851, those government departments that had heard of St Kilda assumed it to be unpopulated.

Although the important needs of the community might be seriously neglected, the trivial were sure to receive every attention. On 1 April 1901 (perhaps it was all a hoax) *HMS Bellona* left Greenock bound for St Kilda and arrived in Village Bay two days later. The captain, escorted by a mixed company of marines and bluejackets, came ashore in a longboat. The standard was raised and at once lowered to half-mast, while in solemn tones the captain announced the death of Queen Victoria and the accession to the throne of Edward VII in front of a bewildered group of St Kildans. The company presented arms, the band played 'God save the King' and bearing away their flag they marched down to the beach and left by the same way as they had come.

The simplicity of the St Kildans has always been a favourite subject for comment, especially with those visitors to the island who could draw sharp contrasts between the sometimes risible naïvety of the natives and their own sophistication. But even in the Outer Hebrides where life was in many respects very similar to what it was on Hirta, the St Kildans had a reputation for being extraordinarily ingenuous. On one occasion, perhaps 200 years ago or more, a party of eighteen St Kildans went over by boat to North Uist to buy some seed-corn. Their visit was a great success with the Uistmen, who thought them very curious people, not only because of their strange way of speaking Gaelic, but because whenever a question was put to one of them all eighteen would answer in perfect unison. When asked whether the sacraments of marriage and baptism existed in St Kilda, the islanders replied: 'Oh my dear beloved, no, we have no marriages or baptisms, rather we are dying

out. How shall we marry and baptize, did not the "bramach-innilt"
die? And we cannot have children, and we are, my dear, like to
die out.' When asked what the 'bramach-innilt' was, for the word
did not exist on Uist, the St Kildans all answered together, 'It is,
my dear, the female who attends to the woman who is sending
children into the world.'

There are a number of similar stories and anecdotes which reflect
the simplicity of the islanders, but most of them are offensively
patronizing. Like children the St Kildans were curious and easily
impressed by anything new, but they were also suspicious of what
they did not understand and therefore readily made fun of. But it
was nonetheless remarkable that as late as 1851, the time of the
Great Exhibition when the paraphernalia of progress was being
displayed to the world, there should have been living in Britain
a community of people who had never seen rabbits, rats, pigs, nor
bees let alone iron-works and railways. Only those who had been
to Skye knew what a tree looked like and had the greatest difficulty
in describing it to their friends at home. When Martin visited St
Kilda in the 17th century the islanders thought reading and writing
the most extraordinary skills and could not really believe that it
was possible to express oneself by making black marks on a white
piece of paper.

Martin also recorded a strange and fascinating account, given
to him by a St Kildan who had been taken on a visit to Glasgow
by some men from Harris. It is quoted here in full:

'Upon his arrival at Glasgow, he was like one that had dropt
from the clouds into a new world, whose language, habits etc., were
in all respects new to him; he never imagined that such big houses
of stone were made with hands; and for the pavements of the streets,
he thought it must needs be altogether natural, for he could not
believe that men would be at the pains to beat stones into the
ground to walk upon. He stood dumb at the door of his lodging,
with the greatest admiration; and when he saw a coach and two
horses, he thought it to be a little house they were drawing at their
tail, with men in it; but he condemned the coachman for a fool
to sit so uneasy, for he thought it safer to sit on the horse's back.
The mechanism of the coach-wheel and its running about, was the
greatest of all his wonders. When he went through the streets, he
desired to have one to lead him by the hand. Thomas Ross, a merchant, and others, that took the diversion to carry him through the
town, asked his opinion of the High Church? He answered that it
was a large rock, yet there were some in St Kilda much higher, but

that these were the best caves he ever saw; for that was the idea
which he conceived of the pillars and arches upon which the church
stands. When they carried him into the church, he was yet more
surprised, and held up his hands with admiration, wondering how
it was possible for men to build such a prodigious fabric, which
he supposed to be the largest in the universe. He could not imagine
what the pews were designed for, and he fancied the people that
wore masks (not knowing whether they were men or women) had
been guilty of some ill things for which they dared not show their
faces. He was amazed at women wearing patches, and fancied them
to have been blisters. Pendants seemed to him the most ridiculous
of all things; he condemned periwigs mightily, and much more the
powder used in them; in fine, he condemned all things as super-
fluous he saw not in his own country. He looked with amazement
on everything that was new to him. When he heard the church-bells
ring, he was under a mighty consternation, as if the fabric of the
world had been in great disorder. He did not think there had been
so many people in the world as in the City of Glasgow; and it was
a great mystery to him to think what they could all design by living
so many in one place . . . when he saw big loaves, he could not tell
whether they were bread, stone or wood. He was amazed to think
how they could be provided with ale, for he never saw any there
that drank water. He wondered how they made them fine clothes,
and to see stockings made without first being cut, and afterwards
sewn, was no small wonder to him. He thought it foolish in women
to wear thin silks, as being a very improper habit for such as pre-
tended to any sort of employment. When he saw the women's feet,
he judged them to be of another shape than those of the men,
because of the different shape of their shoes. He did not approve of
the heels of shoes worn by men or women; and when he observed
horses with shoes on their feet, and fastened with iron nails, he
could not forbear laughing, and thought it the most ridiculous thing
that ever fell under his observation. He longed to see his native
country again, and passionately wished it were blessed with ale,
brandy, tobacco and iron, as Glasgow was.'

Martin was before his time with his account of an Arcadian in
Glasgow. The myth of the noble savage did not really become
popular in England until after 1785, when Captain Cook returned
from his second voyage to Tahiti bringing with him the native,
Omai, who was subsequently feted in all the salons of London.
The desire to return to a simpler life, however, and its attendant

notion that man in a 'natural' state is naturally virtuous, are as old as civilization itself. In the case of St Kilda accounts of the simplicity of the islanders and their primitive way of life inevitably became confused with estimates of their moral worth. Martin, however, was almost blameless in his objectivity; his only fault lay in being the first to write about the St Kildans in detail. Sooner or later the romantic idea of 'lone St Kilda' was bound to worm its way out of obscurity and feed upon the latent idealism of escapees from discontent. By doing his job well Martin merely eased its passage.

If St Kilda was romanticized, it was not entirely without reason. The islanders were undoubtedly paragons of simplicity, but they were also, it seems, in their virtue sublime. They had little aptitude for crime; theft was almost unknown on the island, as were drunkeness and swearing; disputes were easily settled and adultery rare. The first record of an illegitimate birth was in 1862 and after that there were only two more before the evacuation. Nor could the St Kildans justly be accused of being merely free from vice rather than possessed of virtue. The bond of common interest which united them so firmly together created by extension a genuine concern for the welfare of others. Once when a ship was spied off the coast of Hirta weathering under a storm and in danger of foundering on the rocks, the entire community immediately retired to the church and prayed for the safety of the crew. After seven hours the St Kildans were still on their knees. Eventually the wind changed and the ship was able to make an anchorage in Village Bay. Trite enough in themselves, the accumulative effect of such stories (and there are plenty of them) can wear down the resistance of the most sceptical. 'Their morals,' wrote Macaulay in 1758, 'are, and must be, purer than those of great and opulent societies, however much civilized.' In a restricted sense he was right. If morality has its origins in those mores or customs, which enabled the earliest type of village society to sustain and direct itself, then the morals of the St Kildans were certainly closer to this original purpose than those of 18th century city-dwellers living in London or Paris. By the same token it must have been difficult to have led an immoral life in St Kilda—with one's own survival at stake that little bit of evil to relieve the tedium would have seemed hardly worth the effort.

Happily not everyone shared in the general enthusiasm for the noble St Kildans. Lord Brougham, who spent a short time on the island in 1799, described with contempt how : 'A total want of curiosity, a stupid gaze of wonder, an excessive eagerness for spirits and tobacco, a laziness only to be conquered by the hope of the above mentioned cordials, and a beastly degree of filth, the natural consequence of this, render the St Kildan character truly savage.' Although Brougham's reaction was healthy enough he probably misunderstood much of what he saw on Hirta. The accusation of laziness was to be levelled at the islanders with some justification eighty years later, when tourism and charity had taken away the incentive to work, but earlier visitors, like Brougham, sometimes failed to appreciate the different pace of island life and the different outlook of the inhabitants. The suggestion that they would do anything for whisky is probably a fiction, since to the St Kildans, later to become renowned for their abstemiousness, whisky was always more precious as a medicine than as a drink. Their love of tobacco, however, is more plausible. Macaulay wrote of their 'violent passion' for this 'bewitching article', though others denied it in equally strong terms. Certainly supplies of tobacco must have been very irregular and at times it would have been regarded as a great luxury. When there was no tobacco the islanders smoked dried moss, silver weed, and other herbs; if they were eager for the real thing it was not very surprising.

The St Kildans were often accused, in their dealings with visitors, of displaying a certain cunning, especially where barter was concerned, and also of being able to tell a lie with impunity, particularly if it was more a case of withholding the truth. In the second half of the 19th century when the islanders began to appreciate the value of money without fully understanding its consequences, their character suffered; they became spoiled and grasping. But though their innocence was lost, the basic goodness of the people remained, even when the community was at its lowest ebb.

In the halcyon days before the arrival of tourists and money, very few people ever visited St Kilda. Foreigners (anyone who did not speak Gaelic was a foreigner) were regarded as great curiosities by the islanders and usually received with a mixture of fear and delight. 'The islanders in general are unfashionable enough to possess the virtue of hospitality in an eminent degree', wrote Macaulay, and both he and Martin, who themselves were swamped with gifts and kindness, testified that the St Kildans showed a natural concern for the well-being of strangers; taking them into their homes, supplying their needs as best they could and endlessly asking them whether they had slept well or had eaten enough or wanted something. Martin observed that 'Both men and women are very courteous; as often as they passed us every day, they

saluted us with their ordinary compliment of "God save you";
each of them making their respective courtesies'. But the St Kildans
did as much among themselves and it was customary to shake hands
with everybody on the island at least once a day.

The shipwrecks which litter the history of St Kilda were a source
of strangers, who, though not always welcome, were usually well
received. In 1686 a ship-load of French and Spanish sailors were
wrecked off Rockall and made their way to Hirta, where they were
taken in and looked after by the islanders, even though they
offended them by starting work on their boat on a Sunday. According to Martin the natives were 'astonished, and being highly dissatisfied, plucked the hatchets and other instruments out of their
hands and did not restore them till Monday morning'. In 1839
eighteen men from the *Charlotte*, also wrecked off Rockall, turned
up in St Kilda and were given clothes, shelter and food for eleven
days. In 1864 the crew of the *Janet Cowan* received the same treatment, and in 1887 nine men from the Austrian ship, *Peti Dubrovacki* spent nearly six weeks on the island at a time when the
inhabitants were desperately short of food. Ships would sometimes
call in at St Kilda for supplies of water and fresh meat, but their
crews did not always make themselves popular with the islanders.
At the time of Martin's visit the St Kildans were prejudiced against
all seamen as a result of a recent incident where some foreign
sailors had started raping their women, which had shocked them
deeply. They decided that in future they would not allow more than
ten sailors on the island at the same time, and those only if they
were unarmed.

Apart from these chance visitations and the once yearly visit of
the steward, contact with the outside world until the 19th century
remained negligible. In spite of the works of Martin and Macaulay
very few people had heard of St Kilda and of those who had, almost
none were prepared to risk their lives (or so they thought) in getting
to and from so isolated and god-forsaken a place. In some parts
the island still had the reputation of being a penal colony, which it
had acquired long ago from old tales of how the MacLeods used
to get rid of troublemakers by sending them out to St Kilda; and
in more recent times the strange story of Lady Grange had done
nothing to dispel that image.

James Erskine, the brother of Bobbing John, the Earl of Mar
who led the 1715 rebellion in Scotland, was by all accounts a
canny man. Like his brother, Erskine harboured Jacobite sympathies

but hid them, sometimes almost too successfully, beneath an exterior show of loyalty to the Government. In 1707 he was made a judge in the Court of Session and assumed the judicial title of Lord Grange. That same year he also took a wife. Her maiden name was Rachel Chiesley, and it was generally agreed that she was lucky to have made such a good marriage, for she was the daughter of a convicted and hanged murderer. Her father, who had deserted his wife and children, on being ordered to pay them alimony by the Lord President, Sir George Lockhart, had taken umbrage. He objected to what he considered an unjust verdict and showed his resentment by shooting Lockhart in the head as he was coming out of church.

Rachel, now Lady Grange, lived with her husband and a large family in a house in Edinburgh at the foot of Niddry's Wynd just off the High Street. She was a violent woman, prone to ungovernable rages and touched now and then by fits of madness. By 1730 her marriage with Grange, which had never been much of a success, came to an end. Although each blamed the other for the rift, probably with some justification on either side, it was Grange, who, unable to bear the strain of living with his harridan any longer, sent her off to the country with the children and £100 a year to live on. But alimony was not a popular subject in the Chiesley family and Lady Grange resented having to receive it almost as much as her father had objected to handing it out. She disliked the country intensely and refusing to accept her banishment, decided to take her revenge.

Her weapon was a document which showed that although ostensibly a supporter of the Government, her husband was involved in Jacobite dealings. Lady Grange returned to Edinburgh, went straight round to Niddry's Wynd and stood in the courtyard below her husband's window, waving the proof of his treachery in the air, shouting obscenities and screaming to the world at large all the most damning stuff she could remember. Grange deliberately paid his wife no attention and eventually she went away and found lodgings in the city. But she returned to Niddry's Wynd day after day and repeated her performance. Although he received nothing but sympathy from those who witnessed his wife's ravings, Grange realized that she was rapidly becoming dangerous to him. Unable to appeal to the Law to have her removed by order, he turned to the notorious Simon Fraser, Lord Lovat, and certain other Highland chiefs who were worried by what Lady Grange might give away if she were asked the right questions. They at once agreed to help, and a plan to have her sequestrated was formed as quick as anyone could say kidnap.

At a few minutes to midnight on 22 January 1732 a party of Highlanders wearing Lovat's uniform forced their way into Lady Grange's apartment and seized its only occupant. She was treated far from gently, as she herself later testified: 'They threw me down upon the floor in a Barbarous manner I cried murther murther then they stopped my mouth . . . their hard hands bleed and abassed my face all below my eyes they dung out some of my teeth and toere the cloth of my head and toere out some of my hair.' Still struggling she was taken in a sedan chair, which had been waiting in the courtyard below, to the outskirts of the city, where she was transferred with the help of a rope to the back of a horse and galloped twenty miles through the snow, still gagged and bleeding, to the house of John MacLeod at Muiravonside. After dark the party set off again and carried poor Rachel to Wester Polmaise, a house belonging to a man called Stewart, whose factor was one of her captors. Here she spent the next thirteen weeks in a small room at the top of an old tower. Its only window was boarded up and its prisoner was never allowed to see the light of day or breathe the fresh air throughout her stay.

In August Alex Forster of Corsebonny, who had led the kidnap gang, took the captive north into the Highlands and delivered her into the hands of Lovat's own men. After a long and painful journey Lady Grange finally reached the Isle of Heskeir on 30 September. She spent the next two years on the island as a prisoner of its owner Sir Alexander MacDonald of Sleat. Although she was treated more mercifully on Heskeir, being unaccustomed to the Highland way of life, Lady Grange found it miserable. She made a vain attempt to escape by bribing a man to fetch a boat, but unfortunately he absconded with the money, which soon led to her bid for freedom being found out. In June of 1734 a sloop under the command of John MacLeod arrived at Heskeir to take the prisoner to a place from which escape would be impossible.

'Oh alas much have I suffer'd often my skin made black a blew, they took me to St Kilda. John MacLeod is called Stewart of the Island he left me in a few days no body lives in but the poor native it is a viled, nasty and stinking poor isle. I was in great miserie in the Husker (Heskeir) but I am ten times worse and worse here.' She lived in a two roomed cottage some way below the village in the Bay area. A native girl waited on her and the St Kildans saw to it that she had all the food and warm clothing that she needed.

But no one on the island spoke English, there were no books, nothing to do, no crumb of relief from the tedium except for the yearly visits of the steward who sometimes brought her little luxuries. Perhaps in order to avoid the company of the islanders, who despite or even because of their kindness drove her to violence at times, she took to sleeping by day and living by night. She drank as heavily as her meagre supplies of whisky allowed and every night would wander down by the dark shore like a wild swan with a damaged wing, bemoaning her captivity. Gradually madness returned and, rising up as the pitiless Atlantic wind, blew until the dispersal of her senses was complete.

Throughout the seven years she spent in St Kilda Lady Grange made repeated attempts to contact her friends on the mainland. Apart from trying to persuade one of the steward's retinue to accept the promise of a bribe, she could do little more than throw messages into the sea, but eventually she was successful by another method. She managed to hide a letter in a skein of yarn, which was collected as part of the rent by the steward and taken to Inverness. The letter was dated 20 January 1738 but did not reach the Solicitor General, to whom it was addressed, until the winter of 1740. It told in detail of the poor woman's ordeal and ended with the plea : 'When this comes to you if you hear I'm alive do me justes and relieve me, I beg you make all hast but if you hear I'm dead do what you think right befor God.'

The letter, which caused a great stir in Edinburgh, came into the hands of Mr Hope of Rankeillor, Lady Grange's legal agent, who, although a Jacobite himself, felt moved to attempt to rescue her. He applied for a warrant to search St Kilda and liberate its captive, but for some time his application was blocked by Grange's friends before permission was finally refused. Undeterred Hope took a ship of armed men out to St Kilda at his own expense, but he arrived too late. Lady Grange had already gone. She was taken to Assynt in Sutherland and from there to Skye, where she spent the last of her twelve years of captivity and died, a mad woman, in May 1745. Her body was buried at Trumpan in Waternish, while at Dunvegan the MacLeods and their Jacobite friends tempted fate by giving her a mock funeral with a coffin full of earth.

In spite of the exemplary hospitality, which the St Kildans extended to all visitors to their island (whether they were being detained there or had come of their own accord), their attitude towards strangers was complicated by one curious factor. Until the middle of the

19th century the islanders always reacted with alarm to the arrival of strangers and as a preliminary the whole community would disappear into the hills and hide among the rocks. Beside the age-old fear of physical violence there was another still more potent reason for their resentment of foreigners. Due to the rarity of disease among the islanders and their consequent lack of immunity every time a stranger came to the island all the inhabitants would be struck down with illness. This complaint, which came to be known as the stranger's cough or the boat-cold, was like a severe bout of 'flu. It usually began with an aching around the jaw, which spread to all the limbs, and was accompanied by a headache and depression, ending up with a cold and cough. Between 1830 and 1846 there were six deaths from the stranger's cough, but the worst of the disease was that it affected everyone on the island and could put a stop to work for a period of a week or more. If the islanders caught it at an important time of year, during the fulmar season or at harvest-time, it could cause serious hardship.

The St Kilda boat-cold has many parallels on other remote islands like Tristan da Cunha, Pitcairn, Foula and Fair Isle, but for a long time it was not taken seriously and all kinds of theories were put forward to explain it away. The St Kildans were never in any doubt that strangers were responsible, but the strangers liked to look around for other possible causes. Some attributed the illness to the dubious fact that whenever visitors came to the island the inhabitants would rush into the sea to help them with their boats, and thus expose themselves to the cold. Others suggested that it came with the east wind, which they claimed was the most propitious for landing in Village Bay (not true). Some said it was an annual epidemic, others that it was psychosomatic. When Dr Johnson was told about the stranger's cough and how the islanders suffered from it each year about the same time that the steward payed his visit, he remarked, 'The steward always comes to demand something from them, and so they fall a-coughing.' There may have been an element of truth in this explanation, but basically the St Kildans were right, the strangers were to blame. In the last century explorers and naturalists in remoter parts of Africa and South America quite often found that tribes which were friendly with Europeans gradually became extinct. Their resistance to the germs of civilization was so low that any contact with their carriers was enough to make them ill. Regardless of whether the visitors themselves were healthy or not, the natives would develop a slow fever with many of the symptoms of the common cold, which eventually killed them.

As contact with the mainland increased over the years the St Kildans appeared to be less troubled by the boat-cold, though other diseases, many of them previously unknown on the island, took its place. The islanders' resentment of strangers on this account was overridden by their curiosity and love of novelty which only visitors from the world outside could satisfy. Tourists became an important source of income to the community, but the people finally grew tired of being put on display, of having their customs and traditions ridiculed and their way of life pitied. Something of their old fear of foreigners returned, but by then it was too late.

CHAPTER SEVEN

Birds and Cragsmen

'The exercise they affect most is climbing of steep rocks. He is
the prettiest man who ventures upon the most inaccessible,
though all they gain is the eggs of the fowls, and the honour
to dye, as many of their ancestors, by breaking of their necks.'
                    Sir George Mackenzie of Tarbat, 1675

Gannets, solan or spectacled geese were the principal quarry, food
and export of the St Kildans from earliest times until the middle
of the 18th century. Their colony, still the largest in the world, is
concentrated on Boreray and its two main stacs, Lee and Armin, by
way of which Martin first came to St Kilda. 'We arrived there, and
put in under the hollow of an extraordinary high rock (Stac an
Armin), to the north of this isle, which was all covered with a prodigious number of solan geese hatching in their nests; the Heavens
were darkened by those flying above our heads; their excrements
were in such quantity, that they gave a tincture to the sea, and at
the same time sullied our boat and cloaths.' Martin calculated that
the population of the gannet colony could not be less than 100,000,
which is approximately what it is today: in 1960 over 40,000
breeding pairs were counted. In the 17th century the St Kildans
were catching more than 22,000 gannets each year, but by the early
19th century the number had fallen to around 5,000 and by the
1920s only 300–400 birds were being taken. The decline was partly
due to the changing demand from the mainland markets and
partly to the decline of the community itself.

Hunting gannets was always a difficult and dangerous business.
It involved a boat trip across four miles of open sea to Boreray
(there are no gannets on Hirta), which could only be undertaken
in calm weather. A sudden storm or a dense fog were not predic-
table and could be serious hazards. The job had to be done on a
moonless night. Two men with the customary ropes round their
waists climbed up (or if the approach was from above, were lowered
down) the chosen rock face until they reached the ledges where the

gannets were sleeping. It was their responsibility to dispatch quickly and silently the sentinel bird, which kept watch while the others slept. From Martin's account it was upon this exercise that the whole success or failure of the mission depended. Once the sentinel was out of the way it was then comparatively easy to go through the sleeping gannets, knocking them on the head and throwing them down into the sea; 'but if the centinel be awake at the approach of the creeping fowlers, and hear a noise, it cries softly, grog, grog, at which the flock move not; but if this centinel see or hear the fowler approaching, it cries quickly, bir, bir, which would seem to import danger, since immediately after, all the tribe take wing, leaving the fowler empty on the rock'.

According to Macaulay the safety of the flock does not depend on the alertness of one bird but of all of them. The 'grogs' and the 'birs', however, have the same significance and if the fowlers succeed in killing a gannet, and continue to hear the signal of security (grog, grog), they 'advance, and lay with great caution the first Solan-Goose which they kill, among his old companions; . . .the living begin to mourn immediately over their departed friend, with a lamentable tone of voice, examining his body narrowly with their bills, and are so deeply affected, that the fowlers improve their sorrow and confusion, much to their own advantage'. But if the alarm was given and the gannets flew off, the fowlers had to look out for their own safety in case of a rear-guard action. As they left the ledges the gannets would sometimes wheel and attack, beaks like harpoons, carrying off caps and scarves. In the darkness of the night the hunter's eyes were particularly vulnerable. If the venture had been successful the fowlers threw the dead birds down into the sea (on Stac Lee the gannets made this last dive from a special promontory called the Casting Point), where they were picked up by the men waiting in the boat. Some of the gannets were then prepared for storage in cleits on Boreray. A mark was cut into the foot of each goose to show to whom it belonged. The rest were taken back to Hirta in the boat.

Gannets migrate from St Kilda in November and do not return again until the early spring. The first birds start to come back towards the end of January and by the end of March most of them have arrived. This was when the St Kildans used to hunt the old birds. Though not so good to eat as the young gugas, they made a welcome change to the cured food, which the islanders had been eating all winter. Towards the middle of May the St Kildans would make another expedition to Boreray to collect gannets' eggs.

They took the eggs from Boreray itself and all the stacs in the group except for Stac Lee. Since gannets will lay again if their eggs are taken, this meant that the young birds on Stac Lee were ready for harvesting before the others, which gave a double crop and an opportunity for an extra expedition in September, when the second batch of guga were ripe. But in the latter half of the 19th century Stac Lee was climbed for eggs and all attempts at farming the birds were abandoned.

The gannet was gradually replaced by the fulmar as the staple of St Kilda. Even in the 17th century the islanders preferred the fulmar as food and when its feathers and oil became popular on the mainland in the 18th and 19th centuries they learnt to like it even better. 'Can the world exhibit a more valuable commodity?' Macaulay was asked by a St Kildan. 'The fulmer furnishes oil for the lamp, down for the bed, the most salubrious food, and the most efficacious ointments for healing wounds, besides a thousand other virtues of which he is possessed, which I have not time to enumerate. But to say all in one word, deprive us of the Fulmer, and St Kilda is no more.' The fulmar was in many ways a much safer bet than the gannet. It nested in the cliffs of Hirta, stayed in St Kilda all the year round apart from a brief migration from September to November, was easier to catch and, since until 1878 St Kilda had the only breeding colony of fulmar in the British Isles, it gave the islanders a monopoly on its produce.

From the beginning to the middle of May the fulmar lay their eggs, usually on a grassy slope or ledge in the cliffs, and sit on them, both parents taking turns, for the next six or seven weeks. Each hen lays one egg and will not lay again if that egg is removed. 'So exquisitely nice are his feelings,' wrote Macaulay, 'and so strong his resentment, that he conceives an unconquerable aversion for his nest if one breathes over it and will never pay it any more visits : For this reason, to plunder his nest, or to offer indignity to it, is in Hirta a high crime and misdemeanour.' But towards the end of the community's existence the rule was relaxed and fulmar eggs were taken with impunity. After the chick has been hatched the parents feed it for a further seven weeks until it is fully fledged and ready to leave the nest. Then, when the young birds are at their fattest, but just before they have learnt to fly, the St Kildans reap a cruel harvest.

The opening date for the fulmar season fell appropriately on 12 August, or near enough, and lasted for over a fortnight. They were without doubt the most important weeks in the St Kildan calendar.

The following account of a fulmar harvest is taken from the diary of the Reverend Neil Mackenzie :

'During the preceeding week an unusual excitement and alertness pervades the village. Every possible preparation is being made. The women bring the cattle home from the shielings, grind sufficient meal to last the killing time, while the men test the ropes, make good deficiences, and provide barrels and salt.... A large and valued proportion of the winter's food must now be provided or you have to do without it. The breeding-places have all been carefully examined some time before, and an estimate made of the young birds which they respectively contain. They are now divided into as many portions as there are groups of four or five men who are to work together. The portions are now assigned by lot to each group, and all is ready. When the day considered most suitable comes all move off to the rocks, and the men either climb down to the breeding places or get lowered by rope if necessary. The birds must all be caught by hand, and skilfully too, or much of the valuable oil will be lost. They must be caught suddenly and in such a way as to prevent their being able to draw their wings forward or they will squirt the oil. It cannot do this easily while you hold the lower joints of its wings back against each other. Caught in the right way its neck is speedily twisted and broken and the head passed under the girdle. When the man has got strung about him as many as he can conveniently carry, they are passed up to the women who are waiting above. At once they are divided into as many shares as there are men in the group, when the women-kind and children seize upon their shares and begin to drain out the oil into receptacles, which are generally made out of the blown-out and dried stomachs of the Gannet. This they do by the very simple means of holding the bird's bill downwards and gently pressing, when about a gill of oil flows out by the bill.... When all are got home, plucking off the feathers, disposing of the internal fat, and salting the carcases for winter use, goes on till far in the night. Early the next morning the same round begins, and so on from day to day till all the accessible breeding-places are visited. All this time there is nothing but birds, fat, and feathers everywhere. Their clothes are literally soaked in oil, and everywhere inside and outside their houses nothing but feathers; often it looks as if it were snowing.'

Each fulmar carries about half a pint of rust-red oil, which it will spit in self-defence at anyone coming too near its nest. The young birds with a range of two to three feet could sometimes take a fowler by surprise and make him lose his foothold on the cliff-face. The oil is produced by the glands of the proventiculus (when it runs out of oil the fulmar begins to vomit like a frightened heron) and has a musty pervasive smell which is difficult to get rid of. In the 19th century fulmar feathers were sold to the Government for stuffing army mattresses and pillows. They were popular because they discouraged lice and bed-bugs, but the feathers had to be fumigated before they could be used and when after three years the smell returned, the soldiers would insist on their being treated again.

The St Kildans regarded fulmar oil as a sort of panacea. It soothed rheumatic pains, bruised or aching limbs and served as 'a purge and a vomiter'. It was also a chief ingredient of giben, which was thought to be the only possible remedy for the stranger's cough. Rich in vitamins A and D, fulmar oil was sold as a medicine on the mainland; in London and Edinburgh it acquired a reputation as a balm for toothache and sprained ankles. But though the fulmar and its products were always appreciated in St Kilda by the end of the 19th century they had lost much of their appeal abroad. As medicine became more sophisticated fulmar oil went out of fashion, and where it had once been used for heating and lighting, it was replaced by paraffin. Similarly the fat of the fulmar, which had been sold as grease, was superseded by mineral oils. The bird itself ceased to be marketable when refrigeration and improved communications on the mainland made dried and salted foods obsolete. Communications also affected the sale of feathers. It became uneconomical to buy feathers from St Kilda because of the prohibitive cost of transportation. Cheaper and more efficient methods of stuffing mattresses captured the market and fulmar feathers with their offensive odour ceased to sell. In 1902 the last load of fulmar feathers and oil was taken as rent from the St Kildans, but up until the year of the evacuation the islanders continued to catch and eat as many fulmar as they had always done. When the population declined so did the number of fulmar caught, though the ratio of birds per inhabitant remained more or less steady.

By far the most numerous bird species in St Kilda is the puffin, and although numbers have dwindled considerably in recent years (for reasons as yet uncertain) in the days of the community they were several million strong. Variously known as bougirs, coulternebs, Tammie Norries or popes, puffins arrive in St Kilda in March and leave again at the end of August. They breed in burrows, which they dig out of the grassy slopes, especially on Soay and the

Dun, and lay one egg which is hatched by both parents. In summer they strafe the sky with their short and rapid flight like toy doodlebugs. On the ground they have a look of preposterous self-importance. Wrote Macaulay: 'It seems to be conscious of its own beauty, cocking its head very smartly, and assuming great airs of majesty: Its colour is black on the outer parts, and about the breast red and white. The legs are red, and the beak fashioned like a coulter, edged above, most charmingly painted with red and yellow below.'

	FULMAR CAUGHT ON ST KILDA (J. Fisher)		
Years	*Population*	*Fulmar*	*Birds per inhabitant*
1829–43	*c.* 102	av. 12,000	118 (15 years)
1860	*c.* 78	8,500	109
1875	72	9,056	126
1896	73	8,960	123
1897–1900	*c.* 72	av. 7,500	104 (4 years)
1901	*c.* 74	9,600	130
1906–8	*c.* 77	av. 7,700	100
1910	*c.* 78	9,600	123
1911	80	9,600	120
1929	*c.* 32	av. 4,000	125
29 Years	av. 87	*c.* 10,000 p.a.	av. 115

The St Kildans used a variety of fowling techniques to catch puffins. Dogs were specially trained to go down their burrows and let themselves be attacked by the outraged occupants. When the dog emerged from the hole there might be as many as six or seven puffins hanging by their beaks from its coat. The islanders themselves fowled for puffin with both rods and gins. A fowling rod (which could be used to catch most birds) consisted of a 15-foot long bamboo pole with a thin piece of cane attached to the top end, on to which was fixed a running noose made of horse hair and stiffened with a gannet's quill woven into the fabric to make the noose stand out better. Latterly the horse hair was replaced by wire. Before he could use the rod, the fowler had to get within range of the birds by patient stalking. Slowly, he would then inch the rod forward until the noose was suspended in the air above their heads. At the approach of the rod the birds would become uneasy and many of them would fly off—but not all.

The noose hovered, a quick turn of the wrist flipped it over an unsuspecting head and the next moment the victim was on its way in, flapping and squawking and tugging like a fish on a line. The other birds flew away and the fowler moved on. If he was skilled he could catch 200 or more birds in a day by this method.

Fowling gins required less skill than the rod, but were just as effective, if not more so, though they could only be used to catch puffins. A gin consisted of a piece of rope with as many as forty horse-hair nooses attached to it. Tied down at one end and weighted at the other with a large stone, it was laid out flat on some rock which the puffins were known to frequent. The birds would land on the rock and out of curiosity begin to examine the snare with their flamboyant beaks until one of them got a foot caught. The snared bird would then begin to struggle and make enough fuss to frighten away the others. But after a while it would resign itself and lie down quietly. Some of its companions would return. If the caught bird struggled they would fly off again; but gradually they would grow bolder and start poking at the snare once more. Another puffin would step on to a noose. The two prisoners would start to fight, then become still. More birds would land and look at the snare. More would get caught. And so it went on until ten or more birds were snared. A day with a fowling gin might yield 50 puffins, but much larger numbers were not unusual. One woman caught 280 in a day, another 127 in three hours.

The puffin snares, which were made by the islanders, had to be very strong but at the same time fine enough to be unobtrusive. Both qualities are illustrated by the story of the fowler who, while walking barefoot across a rock where he had laid a gin, caught his big toe in one of the horse-hair nooses. He tripped and fell over the edge of the cliff. Luckily the gin was strong enough to hold him and although he had to spend the night hanging by his toe 100 feet above the sea, he was rescued next day. But the fowling gin suffered from a drawback common to all traps. It was an indiscriminate killer, taking breeding and non-breeding birds alike. With a fowling rod it was possible to be more selective, though it is doubtful whether the St Kildans ever did much farming of puffins. In the Faroe Isles the fowlers used to catch puffins (and still do) with a *fleygustong*, an instrument resembling a very large lacrosse racquet, with which they swept the birds out of the sky. The Faroese used it selectively taking only the non-breeding birds and ignoring the puffins with sand-eels hanging down from their beaks like beards—a sure sign that they were feeding young. But their catches were none the smaller. On a good day with a *fleygustong* a fowler could kill as many as 700 puffins, though it was heavy work and could only be done by men.

In St Kilda a part of the puffin season traditionally belonged to the women, and every mid-summer the Queen of St Kilda would lead a party of girl fowlers to Soay or Boreray to spend two or three weeks hunting puffins. The season began with a rite. The first puffin to be caught was not killed, but plucked of all save its wing and tail feathers and then released. Originally the intention may have been to attract other puffins, but it became a superstition that unless this was done bad luck was certain to dog the expedition. The puffins were caught mainly for their feathers, but they were also eaten by the islanders during the summer months. After a day's hunting the women set about plucking their catch. It was hard work and sometimes their fingers became so numb that they had to drag the tougher wing and tail feathers out with their teeth. When they had been plucked the carcases were split open, gutted (the viscera were usually kept and used as manure) and hung up on strings inside the houses, to dry. Often the St Kildans caught many more puffins than they could eat, in which case they were fed to the dogs or the cattle. In the first half of the 19th century between 20,000 and 25,000 puffins were being caught each year, though later on the numbers came down to around 10,000 per annum.

Gannets, fulmar and puffins were easily the most important birds in St Kilda as far as the islanders were concerned, but at different stages in their history other species were also taken both for food and feathers. The guillemot or lavy, as it was sometimes called, was always considered a good eating bird, but its popularity was partly due to its early arrival in spring. It came in February and, like the gannet, its fresh meat was much appreciated after the salted birds of winter. In the last hundred years of the community's existence the islanders only took enough guillemots to supply this need for fresh food in early spring, but in 1814 the feathers of 3,750 guillemots had helped to pay the rent. In those days the lavy population must have been much larger than it is now. In 1960 their numbers were put at 20,000, though in the last ten years they appear to have been considerably reduced by pollution. The guillemot colonies are to be found throughout the St Kilda group, but the largest is on the top of Stac Biorach in the Sound of Soay.

Guillemots were caught at night by a cunning stratagem. A

few weeks after they had returned to the islands in early February, the fowlers chose a reasonably calm day and late in the evening drove the birds away from their ledges. A fowler with a white cloth over his head was then lowered by rope on to each of the principal ledges. There he had to remain as still as salt until just before dawn when the guillemots began to return to their ledges. The home-coming birds would mistake the fowler in his white cloak for a rock covered in guano (which attracts them since they are very sociable) and try to land on him. As they flew in the fowler was able to trap them with his hands at the rate of a hundred an hour until it became light, when the birds stopped coming and the fowlers returned home with their catch. The following evening was an occasion for feasting.

The largest of the birds killed by the St Kildans was the Great Auk or Gare fowl, now extinct but once a common visitor to the islands. It was never seen in St Kilda after 1829, although there is a story that the last British gare fowl was killed off Stac an Armin in the summer of 1840 by a group of St Kildans, who were under the impression that the bird was a witch.

Fowling in St Kilda in all its different aspects required a variety of skills ranging from an extensive knowledge of the behaviour of birds to a steady hand with the fowling rod, but no single ability was more essential than skill at the cliff-face. If a man was no good at climbing then he was no good to the island and most likely did not survive. By natural selection and early training the St Kildans became skilful climbers to a man. As Martin observed, 'necessity has made them apply themselves to this, and custom has perfected them in it; so that it is become familiar to them almost from their cradles, the young boys of three years old begin to climb the walls of their houses'. The islanders grew up without any fear of heights, and by the age of ten or eleven the boys were receiving their education on the cliffs. At sixteen they were fully fledged cragsmen.

In the early days, except where specific co-operation was necessary, fowling was very much an individual pursuit encouraged by personal competition. The fowler would go off on his own with a rope and a stake, dig the stake in at the top of the cliff, attach the rope and lower himself down. But first he would always make a careful examination of the ground at the edge of the cliff where his rope was to hang, making sure that it would not give way and that no loose stones could be dislodged by the movement of the

(a) St Kildan schoolchildren

(b) Two St Kildan children

(c) Sending a letter by St Kilda mailboat in the hope that it would be washed up and found somewhere on the west coast of Scotland was the only way of communicating with the mainland.

c

a

c

(d) Rachel Anne Gillies

(e) Neil Ferguson and Donald MacQueen grinding corn in a quern. The job was usually done by women but they were unwilling to pose for the photograph

d

(a) Dividing the fulmar catch c. 1890

(b) Finlay MacQueen c. 1904 with his daughter and younger brother John who was later killed in a fowling accident

(c) An artist's impression of fowling in 1891

a) Framed between the ruins of a black house (*left*) and a modern cottage (*right*) a iew of cleits. These storehouses continued to be built by the St Kildans until the vacuation

b) Village Bay with church and manse, looking out over the Dun, offered shelter to passing rawlers.

c) The Gillies family outside their cottage *c.* 1890

d) At the end of the 19th century St Kilda tweed became the chief export from the sland

d

(a) Puffin

(b) Fulmar Petrel

(c) Gannet with young 'guga'

(d) St Kilda wren at its nest in the walls of a cleit

(e) Young Soay sheep

(f) St Kilda field-mouse

(g) Fulmar in flight

e

f

g

(a) 28 August 1930—the St Kildans carried their belongings down to the pier in preparation for the evacuation on the following day

(b) The village street as it is today. Three of the houses (not in the picture) have already been restored by the National Trust for Scotland and it is hoped that eventually the whole street will be reclaimed

rope. By working alone he was sometimes able to reach more inaccessible parts of the cliffs, but he needed skill and strength to climb back up the rock with his catch and rod. If he ran into difficulties, he knew there would be no help available.

In the period of decline the method adopted by most of the islanders (some, like Finlay MacQueen 1870–1942, always preferred to work alone) consisted of expeditions of three or four men, which involved fewer risks. Usually two men would remain on top of the cliff and lower the third down by rope until he reached a suitable ledge, when he would cry out 'Leigas!' for them to slacken the rope. Another rope was sometimes used to lower the fowling rod to the man below and pull up his catch when he had killed sufficient birds, but most fowlers used to carry the birds on belts around their waists. When he was ready to come up the fowler yelled 'Tarning nard!' and those waiting above, who could not always see the fowler and if the wind was strong could barely hear him, pulled away on the rope. To cover lower reaches of the cliff it was necessary to make the descent in two stages. Two men would be lowered to a ledge, from which one of them would lower the other further down the cliff with a second rope. Fowling in pairs roped together was a common safety measure. If there was an accident it could cause the loss of two lives instead of one, but usually if a man fell his companion was able to hold him and a life was saved.

More difficult by far than descending the cliffs from above was the art of scaling them from below, which was the only possible way to reach the lowest ledges on the cliffs of Hirta and Soay and to fowl the stacs. But before any climbing could begin a landing had to be made. This was almost the trickiest part of any expedition to those stacs, like Lee, Armin or Biorach, which to the inexperienced eye seem to rise sheer from the water, smooth and unapproachable as pencil leads. The expedition was usually led by the officer, whose privilege and honour it was to be exposed to the greatest danger. For his pains he was given the heroic name of Gingach. He had to land first and leave last. The difficulty of landing, of getting a foot or a hand hold on the slippery rock, was aggravated by the action of the waves (even in the calmest weather there is always a heavy swell), which carried the boat up and down the face of the rock, while it required all the skill of the boatmen to bring her in close without striking. The officer had to wait for a wave to carry the boat up to a good height, then jump for it. He had a rope tied about his waist and if he fell the others pulled him back to the boat, drenched, humiliated perhaps, but at least without obligation to try again. When he or somebody else was successful they would secure the rope and help the others ashore. The ascent of the stac was then carried out Alpine style, but without the help of sophisticated equipment. All the climbers were roped together and took it in turns to lead, in the hope that if the top man fell the others would be able to hold him.

Stac na Biorach and Stac Dona, which both lie in the channel between Soay and Hirta, were considered by the St Kildans to be the most dangerous and difficult to climb of all the stacs. A stage in the ascent of Stac Dona or the Bad Rock, so called because it was supposed to have claimed several lives, is described by Martin: 'It is reckoned no small gallantry to climb this rock, especially that part of it called the Thumb, which is so little, that of all the parts of a man's body, the thumb only can lay hold of it, and that must be only for the space of one minute; during which time his feet have no support, nor any part of his body touch the stone, except the thumb, at which minute he must jump by the help of his thumb, and the agility of his body concurring to raise him higher at the same time, to a sharp point of the rock, which when he has got hold of, puts him above danger.' The material reward for climbing Stac Dona was a mere four extra sea-birds but the prestige gained was considerable. Stac Biorach, on the other hand, although considered the more difficult of the two, carried no reward and at one time any man who failed to climb it did not get a wife, though the law was eventually relaxed. Biorach has only once been climbed by a stranger. R. M. Barrington, an experienced and well-known mountaineer, went up in 1929 and, although he was accompanied by St Kildan guides, very nearly lost his life in the attempt.

Climbing accidents were common enough in the days when risks were taken for risk's sake, though later on they became much rarer. Anyone who did fall or 'go over the rocks' was never seen again, since it was almost impossible to retrieve a body from the foot of the cliffs and there was little chance of it being washed up on the island's only beach in Village Bay. Dramatic stories were frequently told which depicted the dangers of fowling and the heroism of the islanders at the cliff-face. They played an important part in St Kildan life, not only because of their educational value but because they perpetuated the myth of the heroic cragsman, which encouraged the islanders to believe in themselves and their ability to survive.

A favourite story concerns a father and son, who were out fowling together when one of them noticed, as they were about to climb back up the cliff, that their rope was badly frayed. The son, who realized that the rope was still capable of bearing the weight of one, but not both of them, urged his father to go before him. But because he was old and felt himself to be of little use to the community the father wished to sacrifice himself. The boy would not allow it and eventually managed to persuade the old man, who climbed the rope first and reached the top safely; but while his son was climbing up after him the rope gave way. The horrified father saw his body turn red on the rocks below before being covered over by the white edge of the ocean.

In another story two fowlers were descending the cliff on the same rope. The man nearest to the top noticed that above his head, strand by strand, the rope was coming apart. In a moment he realized that if he did nothing they would both be killed and that if he sacrificed himself his friend, who was some way below him, would never have time to climb back up. Taking the only remaining course of action, he drew his knife and cut the rope just below his own feet. His friend plummeted to his death but he managed to scramble to the top of the cliff and, as the rope finally gave way, was grabbed by the neck and pulled to safety.

Neither story leaves any doubt as to the value of a good strong rope in St Kilda. It was the fowler's most important piece of equipment, equalled only by the bonds of friendship, upon which his life also depended, or in the words of the island adage: 'A sheachd beannachd nan cairdean's a lon laidir na feuma—seven fold blessings to our friends and the strong rawhide rope in time of need'. In the 17th century there were three heavy duty ropes made of horse hair with a protective covering of twisted cow hide to prevent wear on the rocks. They were all 24 fathoms (144 feet) long but could be tied together if necessary to form an extended version. These ropes, which were immensely strong and usually lasted at least two generations, belonged to the commonwealth and could not be used without the permission of parliament. On 11 August each year (the day before the opening of the fulmar season) the ropes were brought before parliament for a general inspection. Each rope was tested by four men selected for their strength, who tied one end of the rope to a rock and pulled on the other for all they were worth. If it held, and passed careful examination, it was reckoned to be safe. By the middle of the 18th century the number of rawhide ropes on the island had increased and some of them, at least, seem to have passed into private hands. According to

Macaulay they were the most valuable possession a man could have and were prized as heirlooms, said to be worth as much as the two best cows on the island. Each family also possessed a shorter rope, about ten fathoms long, made entirely of horse hair. These ropes remained in use until the late 19th century, when they were mostly replaced by hemp and manilla ropes, which were imported ready made from the mainland and soon became the standard equipment of every man on the island.

The other essential means of production in St Kilda was the island's boat, which was needed to visit the various islands and stacs of the group for fowling, tending sheep and fishing. The earliest inhabitants probably built their own boats along the lines of the Irish currachs, but, due to the lack of wood, in recorded history the islanders always imported their boats from the mainland or the Hebrides. In the 17th century there was only one boat in St Kilda, which was 16 cubits (25 feet) long and belonged to the commonwealth, though it was divided into sections according to the island's system of property rights. Each individual was responsible for the maintenance of his section of the boat, and in summer had to cover it over with a large piece of turf to protect it from the sun. During winter the boat was kept full of stones to prevent it from being blown away.

In the early 19th century the St Kildans owned a larger boat with a square sail, which they had made themselves out of twenty-one pieces of cloth sewed together. The pieces were all of different sizes and different colours and had been contributed by the boat's twenty-one section-holders, each according to the amount of land, rocks, boat, etc, that he owned. The sheets and reefs consisted of old bits of garter and woollen rope tied together and were almost as motley as the sail. The boat was called *Lair-Dhonn* or the Brown Mare and must have been a fine sight under full canvas. Sadly she was replaced in 1861 by the *Dargavel*, a new and expensive boat, which was given to the islanders by two philanthropic and wealthy men, Mr Hall Maxwell and the Duke of Atholl, who wanted to encourage fishing on the island. But the *Dargavel* was an unlucky boat. In 1862 a fatal accident was narrowly avoided, and in April of the following year she set sail for Harris with eight passengers and £80 worth of produce on board and was never seen again. Because of the dangers involved the boat was rarely used for crossing the sea to the Long Island or the mainland, for although the St Kildans were expert oarsmen in their own waters they had little experience of sailing. They avoided taking risks and consequently boating accidents were uncommon. If the sea looked ugly, as it only too often did, they kept off it.

Storms and sudden squalls are frequent around St Kilda and difficult to forecast. The islanders nevertheless paid careful attention to what they regarded as sure indications of approaching bad weather. Many of these signs verged on the superstitious but others were more straightforward. Martin describes how one of his companions, 'observing the whiteness of the waves attended with an extraordinary noise beating upon the rocks, express'd his dislike of it, as in those parts a never-failing prognostick of an ensuing storm' —an observation which did not require unusual powers. But the St Kildans were also capable of more subtle prediction based on the experience of generations of weather-watching. They never set out on an expedition without taking careful note of the sky and the position of the clouds: for instance, a dark cloud appearing over the south corner of Village Bay always brought a south wind. And if the waves looked high and white in the east part of the bay or if they made a certain noise before they broke on the shore, the boat did not go out. If the fulmar came into land it was a sign that the west wind would not blow, but if they stayed at sea it was anybody's guess. The times of arrival and departure of migratory birds also provided longer-range forecasts. Since the islanders had no compass they took their direction at sea from the flights of birds when familiar landmarks were obscured by cloud or out of sight.

By the late 1870s there were four boats on the island, at least two of which had been given to the community by well-intentioned visitors; but although these boats were new and well equipped they were not tough enough to withstand the kind of treatment regularly meted out by the elements and the St Kildans. Since there was no jetty in those days the boats had to be dragged up and down the storm beach. Both men and women took part in this exercise with one man, who was excused from pulling, shouting out the orders. But in spite of the energy of the labour force the bottom of the boat was not spared. When Robert Connel, a crusading journalist on the staff of the *Glasgow Herald*, visited St Kilda in 1885 he found the island's boats to be in very poor shape. Connel misunderstood much of what he saw in St Kilda and consequently made a poor diagnosis of the island's problems. He was shocked by the egalitarian principles on which the inhabitants seemed to run their lives: 'The four presentation boats which the islanders now possess are simply going to wreck in their hands, and one apparent reason is that they are common property. What is everybody's business is nobody's business, and so the boats are allowed to lie and rot uncared for on the beach.... If a boat is ever given again it should be presented not to the community but to half-a-dozen of the most deserving members.' Taking the symptoms of decay for its cause, Connel was passing judgement on a social system which had worked well for at least a thousand years. If its organizing principles had begun to disintegrate, if the people had become demoralized, the system itself was not to blame. The reasons were more complex but one of them was to be found on the beach along with the rotting shells of the 'presentation' boats.

Fishing was thought by many to be the answer to the island's problems and the presentation boats and other charitable gifts were often intended as an encouragement in that direction. But the history of fishing in St Kilda, although it had its ups and downs, was not impressive. A 16th century account of Hirta mentions that the islanders were not clever enough to catch fish. There were more cogent reasons, however, for their lack of enthusiasm, not the least being that they were not particularly fond of fish. In 1819 Macculloch wrote in his *Description of the Western Islands of Scotland*: 'The neglect of fishing proceeds from the wealth of the inhabitants. They possess already as much food as they can consume, and are under no temptation to augment it by another perilous and laborious employment added to that to which they seem to have a hereditary attachment; while their distance from a market, and the absence of commercial habits, prevent them from undertaking a fishery for the purpose of foreign sale.' There was also the danger that extra produce might encourage the steward to ask for a higher rent.

Nevertheless the sea around the islands provided a great variety and abundance of fish—cod, ling, torsk, herring, mackerel, saithe, lythe, mullet, turbot, skate and conger, to name just a few—and the St Kildans, who were quite competent to catch them, had always done so when they felt inclined. The older men fished mostly with long lines from the rocks near the village using limpets or the flesh of a puffin for bait, but in spring and summer a ban was placed on angling from many of the rocks in case it disturbed the birds. The boats too were used for fishing and several visitors to St Kilda tried to persuade the inhabitants to start a fishery. For a brief moment the idea caught on. In 1860 Captain Otter of the *Porcupine*, who was engaged in an admiralty survey of the area, had bought 16 cwt of fish from the islanders for £16. This relatively easy money caught the imaginations of some of the younger men who thought seriously about the possibility of making a good profit out of fishing. After a lot of deliberation, however, it was decided by parliament that due to the uncertainty of the sea, the lack of proper harbour facilities and the difficulties of exporting fish at a profit, the project was basically unsound.

The St Kildans continued to fish for themselves and sometimes caught and cured enough cod and ling to help pay the rent. But success was circumscribed by the strict religious practices of the islanders. In Victorian times a prayer meeting was held in the church every Wednesday night, at which attendance was compulsory. The meeting soon became a sort of mid-week Sabbath, so that the men not only refused to put the boats out on Saturday and Sunday but would not fish on Tuesday and Wednesday either, which only left three nights a week for fishing and one or two of these could be claimed by bad weather. By the turn of the century the St Kildans had overcome their aversion for fish and were eating more of it, especially since they were getting free supplies from visiting trawlers, but it was never accepted as a proper substitute for sea-birds. This was the basic reason why the fishing industry did not catch on. St Kilda was always a fowling community, a bird culture, first and foremost. Nobody wanted to risk boats and lives on a pursuit which must take second place, whatever the reward or profit.

Although fowling remained at the centre of life until the evacuation, the last skerries of its former prestige were gradually eroded away. As the population of the island declined there were fewer fowlers to catch fewer birds for fewer people. On the mainland the value of sea-bird produce had fallen until it was no longer worth exporting. But even before fowling ceased to be economically justifiable it had lost much of its ancient glory. It was no longer the exalted sport it had been in the 17th century; the honour of dying of a broken neck no longer appealed to the St Kildans. They took fewer risks and fowling, once the arbiter of death, as well as being the support of life, relinquished control of their destinies.

CHAPTER EIGHT

Agriculture

'Many a rich and useful country will not provide itself all that
it wants; but no country can be rich and useful unless it can
provide itself by supplying its own wants, or can purchase what
it requires by the sale of its own products. This certainly is not
the case with St Kilda.'

ANTHONY TROLLOPE, 1878

Hirta is an unusually green and fertile island, due to the large
quantities of guano it receives from its bird populations. The soil,
a rich though shallow loam, when properly managed, gave a good
return on crops; but the climate with its harsh salt-laden winds restricted agriculture, within recorded history, to the most sheltered
part of the island on the south-east declivity of Village Bay. Although farming was a secondary occupation to fowling in St Kilda,
the land provided a substantial part of the islanders' diet and contributed a variety of produce towards the payment of the rent. All
the arable land was contained within the Village enclave and
amounted to between fifty and a hundred cultivated acres, with
a few more lying fallow. The maximum acreage was not being
exploited, but the St Kildans were never anxious to put more land
under cultivation since it would have meant a loss of pasture for
their cattle and sheep, which they considered more valuable than
crops. They were also aware that MacLeod would have seen more
of the profits of increased production than they would have done,
and so they grew what they needed.

'Their arable land,' wrote Martin, 'is very nicely parted into ten
divisions, and these into sub-divisions, each division distinguished
by the name of some deceased man or woman, who were natives
of the place; there is one spot called *multa terra*, another *multus
agris*.' The Latin names of these ancient land divisions, which had
probably survived from Early Christian times, were still in use at
the end of the 18th century, and the arable land was still divided
up into 400 rips measuring approximately 25 feet by 3 feet. Each

family was allocated a certain number of these tiny fields, amounting in all to between four and eight acres of mixed crops, by parliament. After three years the rips were interchanged. The system was basically the same primitive form of land use, known as 'runrig', which operated in many parts of the Highlands and Islands until the 19th century. A family owned its plot of land and looked after it for the three-year period; when the plots were redistributed it received the same amount of land as before, but in a different place.

Early visitors to St Kilda were impressed by the superior quality of the island's agricultural produce and by what Macaulay called 'the singular industry of very judicious husbandmen'. He described how the islanders first turned the ground with the caschrom, then went over it very carefully with a harrow, removing every stone, root and weed. Their harrows were homemade affairs, mostly of wood but with long tangles of seaweed fixed on behind to scatter the earth. Macaulay wrote, 'It is certain that a small number of acres well prepared in St Kilda, in this manner, will yield more profit to the husbandman, than a much greater number, when roughly handled in a hurry, as is the case in the other western isles.'

The main crop was barley, which matured quickly because the summers were so short. It was imported each year as seed by the factor and when sown in April was usually ready for harvesting by 25 August. The harvest always had to be gathered fast in case of storms, which at that time of year can be devastating. The moment the crop was ripe every able-bodied member of the community, including old people and children, helped to bring it in, sometimes working through the night to beat the weather. The barley was never very long in the stem and, rather than cut it, the islanders would pull it up by the roots, which, though it gave more length, was a waste of precious soil. The stems were used for making thatch and for bedding.

The St Kildans also grew corn and oats but not as successfully as the barley, which for a long time had the reputation of being the finest in the west. Oats had to be sown very thick (about twelve bushels per acre) to withstand the gales and rarely yielded more than three times that amount. Potatoes, which became the staple in most parts of the Highlands, never really caught on in St Kilda, and until the blight of 1847 the islanders used to feed a good part of the crop to the cows. After the blight potatoes did not grow so well, and in 1877 a barrel of potatoes weighing 220 lbs would scarcely yield a further 100 lbs after sowing—and those were often of poor quality, made soft by the salt spray which blew over the island.

No serious attempt was made in St Kilda to rotate the crops. The infield was cultivated more or less continuously and although a few acres were left fallow each year the arrangement was probably haphazard. In the absence of an efficient land-use policy manure was essential to the success of crop raising and was regarded as a precious commodity. Seaweed, commonly used as manure in the Outer Hebrides, was not plentiful enough for that purpose in St Kilda. But there were other sources of fertilizer, as Martin noted: 'The chief ingredient in their composts is ashes of turf mixed with straw; with these they mix their urine, which by experience they find to have much of the vegetable nitre; they do not preserve it in quantities as elsewhere, but convey it immediately from the fountain to the ashes, which by daily practice they find most advantageous; they also join the bones, wings and entrails of their sea-fowls to their straw.' The islanders respected and valued the creative power of their excretions and, as Freudians would be quick to point out, since nothing was wasted, there was no wish to hoard.

With the help of the cattle in winter, manure was prepared on the floors of the black houses. It was not as unhygienic or unpleasant as one might imagine. When a fair amount of peat had been burnt on the fire, the ashes and dung were spread over the floor and then covered with earth. This was sprinkled with more peat dust, watered, then beaten and stamped into a hard surface, on top of which several fires were lit. The operation was carried out regularly until spring, by which time the floor had risen four or five feet, making it impossible to stand up inside the house. When it was time to sow the barley the manure was carefully removed in creels and spread on the fields by hand. The crop was manured again when the barley was a few inches high with sooty thatch stripped off the roofs of the houses, which the islanders replaced each spring. But in 1863 when the people were moved into new zinc-roofed cottages, this was no longer possible. The old black houses were kept on as byres for the cattle and manure had to be collected in an open pit behind each house.

When the barley had been gathered it was thrashed by hand and the grain, after being scorched in a pot, was ground in querns. These hand-mills, which were used from earliest times up until the evacuation, consisted of two circular granite stones, roughly 18 inches in diameter, placed flat one on top of the other. The bottom stone was hollowed out to a depth of 5 inches, and had a central iron or wooden pivot on which the top stone rested. The grain was poured in through a little hole in the top stone, which was turned by a wooden handle. By the time the grain had worked its way out at the sides of the quern it was considered to be sufficiently ground. The mill was placed on a sheepskin rug in the middle of the floor and operated usually by two women who sat crossed-legged on either side of it. One poured in the grain, while the other turned the handle. When it had been ground the meal was put through a sieve, made out of a sheep-skin, which had been stripped of wool, stretched on a hoop and perforated with a hot wire. If they worked hard two women could grind and sieve a barrel of meal in a day, but it was a hot, boring job. For comfort's sake the women used to strip to the waist and as they ground away, they would sing slow and melancholy tunes.

In the 1830s the Rev Neil Mackenzie brought agricultural reform to St Kilda. He organized the building of dry-stone walls around the fields to prevent cattle and sheep from spoiling the crops, and persuaded the islanders to divide the land up into larger units and to adopt a new system of drainage. He also introduced the English spade in place of the 'caschrom', a right-angled spade which the St Kildans used to turn the soil instead of a plough. The immediate result of these and other reforms was that for a short time the yield of the arable land was doubled; but it was not long before a decline set in. As the traditional methods of farming, which though primitive had been effective, were replaced by more modern and efficient methods the people seemed to lose interest. They came to scorn the old ways of doing things without learning to embrace the new. In 1877 it was discovered, for instance, that, as far as anyone could remember, the seed-corn on the island had not been changed for more than fifty years. As a result a very poor strain of seed had been allowed to develop, which seriously reduced the yield from the crops—though by this time the St Kildans were importing most of their meal from the mainland. A number of factors were involved in the failure of agriculture, many of them affecting the decline of the community as a whole, but little by little the amount of arable land on the island was cut back until in 1927 only two acres were being cultivated.

As farmers the St Kildans were more interested in and perhaps more skilful at managing livestock than raising crops. After fowling they considered the minding of sheep to be the most important work on the island, not only for economic and epicurean reasons but because looking after St Kilda sheep often bore more resemblance to sport than work. In 1697 there were 2,000 sheep in St Kilda— 1,100 on Hirta, 500 on Soay and 400 on Boreray. The sheep on Soay

and the Dun were of the primitive breed and belonged to MacLeod.
The St Kildans' own sheep on Hirta and Boreray were a mixture
of Soay and a variety of breeds from blackface to four-horned.
While MacLeod's sheep, which remained pure bred, were only
caught for their wool, the improved breed of the islanders were also
killed in autumn for meat. They were said to be very tender and
have a peculiar but delicious flavour.

St Kilda sheep were extremely wild, especially those on the uninhabited islands, and neither the Soays nor the improved breed
could be gathered in the usual manner. At the approach of a man
or a dog they did not flock together but tended to break and make
off in different directions. An ordinary sheep-dog, however skilled,
could do nothing with them. The island dogs, trained to catch sheep
as well as birds, used to run down individual animals and hold them
by the throat until the men came up to relieve them. So that they
would not harm the sheep the dogs' teeth had to be regularly filed
down; their canines were usually removed at the age of six months
with a hammer and chisel. The dogs were good climbers and needed
to be if they were to match the agility of their prey.

In June the St Kildans used to round up the sheep on each of the
islands for wool gathering. All the dogs and most of the islanders
used to take part in this exercise, which was known as the 'Ruagadh'
and involved chasing the sheep round and round the island until
they were trapped either on a ledge or in front of a precipice. It was
hard work and sometimes rather wasteful since the sheep would
often jump to their deaths rather than be taken, but as far as the
St Kildans and their dogs were concerned the excitement of the
chase was worth it. Many outsiders thought this method of sheep
farming inefficient, but efficiency as a criterion could easily be mis-
applied in St Kilda if it failed to take into account the social as well
as the economic function of work.

The islanders never used shears on either the Soay or their own
sheep; instead they 'rooed' or plucked the wool with the help of a
penknife. Visitors to St Kilda mistakenly regarded this practice as
cruel. It was in the case of the Soay and near Soay sheep just the
opposite. Being at an intermediate stage of domestication the Soay
sheep has acquired a fleece which obscures but does not completely
replace its original coat of hair. If they had been sheared, the Soays
would have lost both the wool and the hair coat and could not have
survived the winter. The wool coat, which becomes quite loose in
summer, can be removed painlessly. In later years the St Kildans
gave up trying to catch the Soay sheep and would simply collect

their wool off the ground, when it had come away of its own accord. Most of the crossbred sheep, however, could have been clipped without any problems, but in spite of attempts to introduce shearing to the islanders they preferred to use the old method of 'rooing' up until the evacuation. George Murray, who, while an undergraduate of Aberdeen University, spent a year in St Kilda from 1886–7 as a school-teacher, recorded in his journal his own attempt to instruct the St Kildans in the use of the shears:

'28 May 1887—The sheep are to be clipped today. I clipped seven yesterday and learned them the way to use the shears. Their shearing instrument is the common knife which of course makes work. One man last year got a pair of shears in a present and on my making use of it yesterday it became an object of wonder and was called a *great invention*. There was a crowd of about forty men and women in a circle round about me with eyes full wide with astonishment at the strange operation which the beast was undergoing. Remarks such as the following were made: "O Love don't cut the throat. Don't take out the liver." While the owner of the beast said it would not stay on that side of the island after hearing such "ghogadich" noise about its ears, meaning the sound of the shears.'

When the wool had been gathered it was spun into yarn by the women, who would sit together and talk or sing as they worked at their spindles. The yarn was woven into a coarse broadcloth by the men, who were all accomplished weavers and would work by night on the looms, which were set up in the houses during the winter months. From mid December till mid February they worked hard at the weaving, sometimes continuing into the early hours of the morning, while the women worked even harder at the preparatory stages. The final process of shrinking the tweed was also done by the women, but when it was to be made up into clothes the men took over. The remaining material was stored until summer for the steward to collect for export.

Before it was woven the yarn was usually oiled with the fat of sea-birds and dyed either with indigo, bought from the steward, or with crotal, a grey lichen, which the women scraped off the rocks. Crotal gave a deep fox colour similar to that of standard Harris tweed. A variegated effect was achieved by tying pieces of string around the hanks of wool, which when removed, left undyed bands. Sometimes the St Kildans dyed the tweed after it had been woven, but they were not masters of the art of dyeing and the steward, rather than risk a botched consignment, preferred to take the tweed intended for export in its natural state.

As the products of fowling began to lose their value on the mainland St Kilda tweed became the chief export from the island. It promised well as an industry and the people received help and encouragement from the proprietor. In 1879 there were thirty-six spinning wheels on the island and a wooden loom in every house all provided by MacLeod. St Kilda tweed, which was like a rougher version of the already fashionable Harris tweed, enjoyed a certain vogue partly because of this similarity and partly due to the romantic image of its own brand name. When the tourist trade got under way the islanders were able to sell tweed, as well as gloves, socks and scarves knitted by the women, direct to the visitors. But the bulk of the material went to the factor, who in 1885 was paying the islanders 3s per yell (48 inches) for tweed and rather less for a coarser blanket cloth which they also produced. When the yell or the 'big yard' was replaced by the 36 inch variety, the islanders made a better profit, but even so the return on labour was pitifully low.

For a time the St Kilda tweed industry looked like being a success. The factor was able to sell a lot of tweed in Stornoway, where it was thought to be ideal for making clothes and retailed as off-the-peg suiting, and also in Glasgow where the St Kilda myth flourished. In 1892 one of the islanders, called Alexander Ferguson, left home and set himself up as a tweed merchant in Glasgow, selling among others his own tweed. But as the market became more competitive St Kilda tweed could not keep pace with its rivals. Transportation costs from Hirta were higher than from other Hebridean islands and St Kilda tweed was not of good enough quality to be priced up to meet the extra overheads. Nor could the proprietor undercut the market by selling St Kilda tweed cheap, or he would have been unable to give the islanders a worthwhile return on their labour. As it was, in 1914 the people were not earning more than $1\frac{3}{4}$d per hour on work devoted to making tweed.

Other islands did better because they had larger populations and could produce tweed under what were almost factory conditions compared to the primitive state of the St Kildan industry. In 1928 the islanders were still exporting 1,200 yards of tweed a year, as the only payment they could offer in return for the increasing number of imported goods they required. But by then St Kilda tweed, which had always sold more on its name than its quality, was no longer fashionable. Even among the homespun idealists, what little demand for it had once existed, fell away. The last attempt at making St Kilda economically viable had come to nothing. The tweed industry had helped to extend the life of the community unnaturally. Its failure merely marked the terminal point of a downward spiral, along which the agrarian economy of the island had already run its course.

The decline of agriculture in St Kilda was self-perpetuating. As fewer crops were grown, less food and bedding were available for livestock; as fewer livestock were kept, less manure was available for crops. In 1697 Hirta had supported just under a hundred head of cattle. They were small, fat and tender animals, and though the majority were the islanders' own some of them may have belonged to MacLeod, who in those days used to pasture his cattle on the island. This would explain the sudden drop to forty head in 1758, and possibly the rise again to ninety head in 1824. But the significant fall in numbers was from fifty in 1877, when the animals were still in good condition and fetching £3 15s per head in the mainland markets, to fourteen sad looking beasts at the time of the evacuation. It was during these last fifty years that feeding the cattle became a problem and the islanders had to pull up grass for them by hand to augment their meagre diet. In summer the cows were pastured in Gleann Mor and the women would walk over from Village Bay morning and evening to milk them. On a calm day the shrill sound of their voices as they called their cows by name could be heard all over the island. They took bundles of grass with them to keep the cows quiet while they were milking. Sometimes they would spend the night there in the old beehive houses which had long been used as shielings, and in the morning each woman would carry back two pails of milk instead of one. If there was any milk left over after everyone had had their share, it was mixed with ewes' milk and made into cheese. Formerly the islanders had been able to export cheese in large quantities, but as the number of cows was reduced they consumed most of it themselves.

Another important factor in the decline of agriculture was the loss of the island's horses. In Martin's time there had been eighteen small, reddish ponies on Hirta, used mainly for carrying peat and stores. By the middle of the 18th century their number had fallen to ten, and over the next hundred years they dwindled to two old nags, which were eventually taken off the island because the St Kildans resented the amount of grass they ate. In other parts of the Hebrides horses were often kept as status symbols, whether there was work for them or not. What work they did do consisted of carrying peat down from the hills and transporting seaweed from the shore to the fields. In St Kilda, where the manure was taken from the houses and easily carried in creels down to the cultivated strips (which lay below the village), the really important function of horses was peat-hauling.

In the absence of wood, apart from the occasional driftwood washed up on the narrow strip of beach in Village Bay, peat was the St Kildans' only fuel. The deposits were mostly to be found in places which were far from the village and an effort to get to: on the tops of hills and up at the north end of the island by the Cambir. As long as there were horses on Hirta there was no problem. They carried the peats from the hags to the cleits, where they were dried, and from the cleits down to the village. But when the horses went and the St Kildans were forced to fetch and carry the peats themselves, they took to burning turf instead. Turf was easier to dig, lighter to carry and could be found much closer to the village, but it gave out less heat than peat and burned for a shorter period. The islanders were soon stripping large quantities of turf from good pasture and land which might have been cultivated. The grass did not grow again on the exposed earth or rock and by the end of the 19th century several hundred acres had been lost in this way.

Although it was quite obvious that they were doing more damage to the land than a large herd of horses, the St Kildans wilfully resisted any attempt to persuade them to start digging peats again. In 1879 Prof M. Forster Heddle, an eminent geologist, visited St Kilda and tried to explain to the islanders how much harm they were doing by removing the turf. He was not a man to mince his words and probably berated them for being lazy. The St Kildans, however, took their revenge. In a letter to a friend the Professor described how, on leaving the island, '. . . they pitched me out of a boat in the getting off when I was looking after the ladies—reduced a specimen of the peat which I was bearing to a pocketful of pulp a little thicker than porter, ruined my aneroid, rusted my steel measure, gave me one wet skin and two broken shins'.

Eventually the St Kildans consumed most of the turf near the village and ended up going as far afield to find turfs as they had once gone to fetch peat. But they refused to see the contradiction or even the seriousness of the situation. It did not matter to them that they might just as well have been digging peat as turf, or that a few horses could have saved them a lot of trouble. As they trudged over the hill in single file struggling under their heavy creels of fuel, sometimes standing out against a white background of snow like an eternal column of refugees, their belief in the inevitability of it all grew only stronger.

CHAPTER NINE

Missionaries and Disease

'A minister for the Islands of the Blest.'   ANON

Organized religion came to St Kilda in 1705 with the arrival of the first permanent missionary to the island since the days of the Culdees. His name was Alexander Buchan. Sent out by the Church of Scotland as a catechist Buchan stayed on Hirta for a period of four years. His claims of success, however, in converting the natives induced the newly formed Society for Propagating Christian Knowledge to have him ordained and sent back to St Kilda to carry on the good work. This time he remained until his death in 1730. While he was on the island Buchan took it upon himself to improve the lot of the St Kildans. He built himself a manse and with money and support from charity started a mission school and the St Kilda free library. His wife furthered the cause by teaching the women how to knit. It was the beginning of the islanders coming to terms with civilization. But if Buchan's incumbency was a success, at least from the Church's point of view, it was not followed up. Over the next hundred years a number of missionaries and ministers were sent to St Kilda, but few stayed long in what was scarcely a desirable benefice, while the gaps between their various terms of office were wide.

When the Rev John MacDonald of Ferintosh visited the island in 1822 he found little which corresponded to his idea of organized religion. Buchan's manse had long ago disintegrated from lack of use and so had most of his teaching. But Macdonald, known and revered as the 'Apostle of the North' for his work in the Highlands, was a puritanical hard-necked evangelist. If Buchan had started something in St Kilda, his influence was never so keenly felt as that of the 'Apostle', who earnestly set about the destruction of the island culture with all the zealous goodwill of a holy bigot. Although he only made four short visits to the island, MacDonald did not waste any time or spare his energies while he was there. During his first eleven days in St. Kilda, which unfortunately coincided with harvest-time, he preached to the inhabitants thir-

teen long sermons. The St Kildans took to this kind of punishment
with enthusiasm and were filled with admiration for the man who
meted it out. They lavished presents upon him and wept bitterly
when he left them for the last time in 1830. But their admiration
and respect were not returned. MacDonald was appalled by the
moral condition of the islanders. 'Swearing is too prevalent among
them,' he wrote, 'and its common expressions, such as by the
sould, by Mary, by the book ... seem to be quite familiar with
them, on every occasion ... it grieves me to say and I took pains
to ascertain the truth that among the whole body I did not find
a single individual who could be truly called a decidedly
religious person.' But it was precisely because of their deep
religiosity that MacDonald was able to lay his dogma over them
so successfully and play upon their superstitious natures until they
adopted its tyranny without question.

The power that a missionary could wield over St Kildan society
was considerable. His education, literacy, knowledge of English, his
experience of the world and a more sophisticated technology set
him apart from the islanders, who happily acknowledged his superiority, encouraged it even. The missionary was never accepted as
an ordinary member of the community. He did not receive a share
in its property or its produce; he could not be a member of its
parliament. Nor did his elevated position make him unequal in an
equal society, since it more or less excluded him from that society.
Nevertheless his easy influence over the minds and hearts of the
people enabled him to control their lives by establishing a theocratic
prerogative. In spiritual matters his word was law and as the old
natural religion, which had been so intrinsic to the life of the community, was gradually dislodged and replaced by dogmatic Christianity delegated from outside, his authority spread with this new
faith into every sphere of human activity.

If the islanders themselves had been aware of this change they
probably would not have resented it, for as far as they were concerned the missionary was a man of God, who could only do them
good. In practical matters his beneficence and usefulness were often
apparent. He was in touch with the mainland and could intervene
there on the islanders' behalf. He could also come between them
and their landlord if there was a dispute. Very often he was their
schoolteacher, doctor and missionary rolled into one. To have
resented so valuable and diverse an influence would not only have
been heretical, it would have been foolish.

Not all the missionaries to St Kilda were men of ability and wide experience, who were willing to concern themselves with the material well-being as much as the spiritual health of their flock. The Rev Neil Mackenzie, who came to Hirta on the 3 July 1830 as the friend and successor to the Apostle of the North, was something of an exception. He worked harder than any man to raise the islanders' standard of living and although his reforms eventually did more harm than good, they did produce results in the short term.

He not only reorganized farming in St Kilda but, after a battle against the forces of conservatism, managed to persuade the islanders to rebuild their village. He received encouragement in this from an English philanthropist, Sir Thomas Acland, who had visited St Kilda in his yacht in 1830 and, having expressed horror at the low standard of housing, left a prize of twenty guineas for the first man to build himself a new home. The new village with its improved black houses was a success, due largely to the efforts of Mackenzie, who even introduced the idea of hygiene and persuaded the islanders to be tidier in their ways and to raise the level of their existence up off the floor by means of beds, chairs and tables.

Soon after his arrival on the island Neil Mackenzie began the building of a new church and manse on the north-east side of the bay about 200 yards from the village. With the help of workmen from the mainland he completed the job at a cost of £600; the money had been raised by MacDonald of Ferintosh. The church, which is still standing today, is a large plain building (30 feet by 18 feet) with four simple gothic windows, a main door facing east and a side entrance for the minister opposite the manse. Inside the atmosphere was dank and depressing. On the earthen floor six pews made of rough deal stood before an altar and an enormous pulpit. Some years later two specially enclosed pews were added, one for the elders, the other for visitors. A pair of wooden chandeliers hung from the ceiling each with three sheep's tallow candles, which gave a feeble flickering light. Just below the church stood the manse, a single storey, slate-roofed house with four rooms, surrounded by a high wall, which protected both the house and its little enclosed garden from the wind and sea. The rooms of the manse were as forlorn and damp as the church. When there was no minister on the island the house stood empty.

Despite his many other commitments, Neil Mackenzie did not neglect the execution of his religious duties. He introduced three services on Sundays and held an evening service in the church every Wednesday. He also called a meeting on Tuesdays in one of the houses to explain the Shorter Catechism. He preached to the

islanders with great skill and used all the techniques of revivalism
to whip up his audience and kindle a kind of hysterical fervour in
their hearts. Malcolm MacQueen, an Islander who later emigrated
to Australia, wrote down his reminiscences of life in St Kilda during
Mackenzie's time : 'One Wednesday night there was a meeting in
the church and I remember hearing Mrs Gillies crying. There were
nine or ten men in the meeting. I afterwards heard one of the men
telling some who were arriving with the boats from their day's work,
"I believe the Spirit of God was formed upon our congregation
tonight". This was the beginning of the revival.' The revivals had
in fact been started by the Apostle of the North. Mackenzie was
doing no more than carrying on where he had left off with this
extremely effective means of bringing a lapsed congregation back
into the fold.

With the help of the Gaelic School Society, Neil MacKenzie and
his wife tried to reinstate education on the island. They began a
daily school to teach reading, writing and arithmetic and a Sunday
school for religious instruction. The St Kildans were happy to learn
and it was not unusual to see three generations of the same family
at their lessons. Mackenzie worked tirelessly for what he had every
reason to believe was the good of the islanders. He confronted them
with change and the notion of progress and in many ways advanced
their material prosperity. Under his guidance the people came
through a period of transition successfully, but the pressure for
change had not come from within the community itself, and when
Mackenzie went away in 1844 he left behind a vacuum, a newly
created dependency.

There followed an interregnum of ten years, when the island
was again without a minister. On the mainland the Free Church
was busy establishing itself after the split with the Church of Scotland in 1843, but it eventually took over the parish of St Kilda and
in 1853 sent out the catechist, Duncan Kennedy, as missionary.
From now until the evacuation the Free Church was to attend to
the spiritual needs of the islanders, but not surprisingly it had difficulty in finding able ministers who were willing to spend time in
so lonely, insignificant and basically unrewarding a parish. As a
result the men who were sent there were not from the first rank.
Only one of them managed to fill the vacuum created by Neil
Mackenzie—not with enlightened leadership, but with blinkered
despotism.

The Rev John Mackay, formerly a school teacher, who had been
ordained expressly for the purpose of going to St Kilda, was an

unmarried man of about fifty, with an alarming capacity for zeal. Shortly after his arrival on the island in 1865 he established a vibrantly harsh rule over his parishioners. Services on Sundays at eleven, two and six o'clock were made to last from two to three hours each, so that effectively the islanders spent the whole day in church. During the week a service, prayer meeting or period of religious instruction was held every day except Monday and Saturday.

Mackay preached long, repetitious sermons in Gaelic, which invariably included the same message of hell-fire and eternal damnation to all sinners. Complete attention was demanded throughout these dim effusions, even of the very young. Children were brought to church from the age of two and trained to keep absolutely still and silent. If they made a noise they were hurried out, but if a child or even an old woman fell asleep during a sermon Mackay would stop, and there and then in ringing tones warn the offender that they could expect no sleep in the next world. To get a point across the minister would often preach several times on the same subject. Between 26 December 1886 and 10 January 1887, a period of two weeks, he preached nine sermons on the Prodigal Son. The stuff of his oratory was borrowed from works like Baxter's *Call to the Unconverted*, Smith's *Moral Sentiments*, Harvey's *Meditations among the Tombs* and the *Select Works of Dr Chalmers*, which bent the shelves of his meagre library. George Murray, the school teacher, charitably described Mackay's sermons as 'poor feeding for the people or, rather, good food spoiled in the serving out'.

Under Mackay's rule the observance of the Sabbath, which had always been taken seriously in St Kilda, was carried to extremes. No work of any kind was allowed on a Sunday; no water could be drawn; no cow or ewe could be milked. Conversation between the islanders was forbidden from Saturday evening until Monday morning; any important communication had to be made by whisper. Singing or whistling was a serious sin. 'The Sabbath is indeed a day of intolerable gloom,' wrote John Sands, the M.P. and journalist who visited the island in 1875. 'At the clink of the bell the whole flock hurry to the Church with sorrowful looks and eyes bent upon the ground. It is considered sinful to look to the right or to the left.' The worst aspect of Sabbatarianism was that it not only prevented work on Sunday and the Saturday before, but also on Wednesday, the night of the prayer meeting, and the preceding Tuesday. Whenever the men went on a fowling or fishing expedition to Boreray or Soay they had to take one of the elders with them, both as a good-luck charm and in case they were stranded and could not get back in time for church on Sunday. But the St Kildans needed little persuading to indulge in superstitious excess, even if it was to their own detriment.

One Saturday in early May of 1877, when there was a severe food shortage on the island, the gunboat HMS *Flirt* arrived in Village Bay carrying relief supplies for the islanders. At 9.30 p.m. the *Flirt* cast anchor and the captain came ashore in a tender. He was met by the minister at the head of a posse of elders, who told him that 'as the people must be prepared for the devotions of the morrow, they could not think of encroaching on the Sabbath by working at the landing of the goods'. After Mackay left St Kilda in 1889 there was a slight improvement, but as late as the 1920s the islanders were going to church twice on Sundays, on the first Monday of every month and to a prayer meeting every Tuesday, with each service putting a stop to all work twelve hours either side of it.

The Rev Mackay received a stipend of £80, most of which came from the Free Church, though the islanders themselves had to contribute up to £20 each year to the Church's 'Sustenation Fund'. On this salary Mackay was able to afford a housekeeper, a native St Kildan called Anne MacDonald. She was a troublesome woman, six feet tall and the scold and terror of the island. She had an unpleasant habit of hissing between closed teeth and worked hard behind the scenes to create discord among the islanders. Ironically they responded by electing her Queen of St Kilda, though she was far from being the most beautiful woman on the island. In her own way she was as bigoted as Mackay himself, over whom she exerted considerable influence. When a stove was given to the people for the purpose of heating the church, she refused to allow it inside the building because she thought it sacrilegious, and insisted that it be left to rust on the porch of the manse.

The minister and his housekeeper made a formidable couple and the people were not unnaturally cowed under their grim rule. Happiness was actively discouraged. Children were forbidden to play games and even made to carry bibles under their arms wherever they went. A draughts board and some picture books brought out for the children by a visitor in 1870 were censored on account of their profanity and not allowed on to the island; and when the young girls were offered educational books by another visitor they refused them and asked for religious works instead. Considering that all the education they received from Mackay was of a religious nature their attitude was hardly surprising.

The minister came in for a lot of criticism from contemporary writers. Wrote Sands: 'The weak-minded pope and prime minister rolled into one, who rules the destinies of the island, has reduced religion into a mere hypocritical formalism, finding no place in his creed for self-reliance or any of the manlier virtues. . . . It is nothing to Mr Mackay whether the poor people starve their crofts or neglect the fishing so long as his own silly fads are observed.' Mackay left St Kilda in October 1889 after twenty-four years as minister. Even he may have realized that he had been there too long. 'I think it is time I was leaving them now,' he said, looking down at his watch, the only one on the island and long ago come to a stop.

Despite the Draconian restrictions and regulations which Mackay imposed upon all aspects of island life, during the last five years of his regime an education which could almost be described as formal, was for the first time made available to the inhabitants. Until then education had been a haphazard affair consisting mostly of religious instruction and entirely left in the hands of the resident missionary. When the charity school was founded in 1709 by Alexander Buchan the people were totally illiterate; by 1830 there had been little improvement, with only one person on the island who could read. But in 1884 the Ladies' Association of the Highland Society raised the money to send the first school teacher to St Kilda. Over the next four years six teachers came and went, Mackay managing to make their lives very nearly impossible; but nevertheless progress was made. By 1888 the school was attended by fourteen children (ten boys and four girls) who assembled nearly every day to learn English, geography, history, arithmetic and composition. One boy was doing well enough to be taking Latin as an extra subject.

At the turn of the century a new wing was built on to the church at MacLeod's expense to be used as a school-house and in 1906 with the arrival of Mr and Mrs MacLachlan, a competent husband and wife teaching team, education in St Kilda began to look as if it had a settled future. By now most of the twenty-two children on the island could speak good English and whereas previously the school had operated only on those mornings when the children were not required to help in the fields, it now became a regular affair from 10 a.m. till 4 p.m. each day with an hour's break for lunch. One of Mrs MacLachlan's chief ambitions was to teach the girls how to sew. She felt strongly that the men should be relieved of their traditional role as tailors of the island. Neil Mackenzie's wife had tried to achieve the same result seventy years before, but neither was successful.

Most of the ministers and teachers who attempted to educate the St Kildans shared the view, which prevailed in Western Scotland throughout the 19th century, that Gaelic was a bar to progress. The principal battle was to teach the islanders English. At one time the St Kildans had been as isolated linguistically as they were geographically. Until the beginning of the last century they spoke a dialect of Gaelic with many words and expressions (probably of Norse origin) which could not be understood by people from the mainland or other islands. They also spoke with a strange lisp and were unable to pronounce liquid letters correctly. Increased contact with the mainland, however, eradicated many of these peculiarities and though a handful of words continued to be pronounced differently to standard Gaelic and some variations in meaning survived, only by their lilting lisp, which never disappeared, could the St Kildans readily be distinguished from other Gaelic speakers.

The St Kildans were not good linguists and even showed a pronounced dislike of foreign languages. They resisted learning English, perhaps as a form of self-preservation, until late in their history. In 1877 apart from the minister there was only one person on the island, a mainland woman from Ross-shire, who could speak English. When they did succeed in learning it, English enabled them to talk in greater depth to visitors and tourists and find out more about the outside world. Inevitably it helped, as did all the education which the islanders received, to raise and nurture tendrils of discontent. Whether or not it would have been possible to educate the St Kildans in terms of remaining on their island, no attempt was made to do so. Education meant finding out that life in the world promised better things. As early as 1888 most of the school children wanted to leave when they were grown-up, and most of them did.

After Mackay's long and tyrannous reign, the Free Church, whether by accident or design, took to sending younger ministers to St Kilda for shorter periods of time. Mackay was succeeded by the Rev Angus Fiddes, an understanding and broadminded man, whose greatest achievement was to control the endemic disease of infant tetanus which had plagued the island for more than a century. He also curbed some of the excesses of Sabbatarianism and reduced the number of services on Sundays to one in the morning and one at night, though, like his predecessor, he was a keen pulpiteer and his sermons could make a service last up to four hours. As a result the islanders still spent at least half the day in church on the Sabbath, but they would have felt cheated by less.

As more enlightened missionaries came and went the oppressive cloud of salvationism lifted a little, but the work of men like Mackay and the Apostle was never to be undone. The imposing of a strict, puritanical orthodoxy upon a people whose simple and vulnerable culture was delicately balanced within the complexities of a natural system, was as successful from one point of view as it was irredeemable from the other. The St Kildans made no attempt to resist the dogmatism which was forced upon them, and even as they watched it bring life on the island to a halt they accepted it as inevitable and right. They allowed fatalism to come uppermost and relaxed into deepest superstition, while their incentive for survival grew weak before the onset of disease and a lingering population crisis.

In the days when they lived in almost total isolation from the rest of the world the St Kildans had been a strong and healthy race afflicted by few diseases. 'They never had a potion of physic given them in their lives,' wrote Martin, 'nor know anything of phlebotomy; a physician could not expect his bread in this commonwealth.' The only medicines they used were their two catholicons, giben, which they took so often with their food that it can have had little value as a medicine, and whisky, a bottle of which was kept in the wall of every house. But as contact with civilization increased the health of the islanders declined. They became susceptible to diseases previously unknown in St Kilda and by the 20th century a general debilitating weakness had set in. They suffered more and more frequently from colds, coughs, headaches and rheumatism, while dyspepsia, scrofula, ear disease and dysentery soon became common complaints. The islanders acquired a taste for medicines and before long the proprietor was sending out a regular supply of castor oil, senna pods, tonics (including the highly popular Gregory's Mixture) and various salts, ointments and bandages. Pills, however, took a little getting used to. In 1860 when the doctor on board the visiting ship HMS *Porcupine* made up some pills for a sick islander, he rejected them on the grounds that they did not constitute 'a fit dose for a grown man'. Contemporary opinion put the ill-health of the St Kildans down to their peculiar diet and hard way of life, but it failed to take into account that the diet and lifestyle of the islanders had changed little over the centuries.

The disease which contributed more than any other to the decline of the community was known on the island as the 'sickness of eight days' because it killed newborn infants usually within eight days of birth. Lockjaw or tetanus infantum was first recorded in St Kilda in 1758 by Macaulay, who described the symptoms: 'On the fourth, fifth or sixth night after their birth, many of them give up sucking; on the seventh their gums are so clenched together, that it is impossible to get any thing down their throats; soon after this symptom appears, they are seized with convulsive fits, and after struggling against excessive torments, till their little strength is exhausted, die generally on the eighth day.' How or when the virus was first introduced to St Kilda is not known, but throughout the 19th century the disease was endemic and its grip on the community tightened as the century progressed. During the period 1830–46 there were 68 deaths on the island, of which 37 were infant deaths; 32 of these (23 male and 9 female) were caused by tetanus. Between 1855 and 1876 there were 64 deaths on the island, of which 41 (26 males and 15 females) were infants: all but 4 had died of tetanus. In that same period there had been 56 births (32 male and 24 female): 15 children (6 male and 9 female) survived. At that time approximately 8 out of 10 children born on St Kilda died of tetanus.

The graveyard filled with infant corpses and preparations for a birth in a family came to include a small coffin. The St Kildans accepted the sad decrement of life as inevitable. They were encouraged to do so by the missionaries, who told them that it was the will of God, his way of punishing the wicked, of keeping the population under control. In reality the disease was decimating the population and taking heaviest toll of the male children who were so important to the survival of the community.

When the Rev Angus Fiddes came to St Kilda he determined to bring the 'sickness of eight days' under control. He appealed to the Scottish Board of Health in Glasgow for help. They sent a nurse, Miss Chishall, who stayed on the island for ten months but achieved little, largely because she was unable to break through the barriers of custom and superstition which the islanders had erected around the secret and mysterious business of birth. After Miss Chishall's departure the Board of Health were unable to find a replacement prepared to go into voluntary exile on Hirta. Fiddes decided to approach the problem himself. He went to Glasgow, where he consulted a number of doctors and medical authorities and took a course in midwifery, which included instructions on the best way to treat the umbilical cord with antiseptic applications after it had been severed—for it was here that the trouble was believed to lie.

On his return to St Kilda Fiddes had great difficulty in persuading the people that his recently acquired knowledge might be of some use. He had to fight long and hard to get the island's midwife, or 'knee-woman' as she was called, to accept his new methods. For centuries it had been her duty to carry out certain rites on the navel of the infant, which involved smearing it with a mixture of fulmar oil and dung. It was thought that the tetanus germ might breed in the old gannet stomachs in which the fulmar oil was kept, but since no outsider (including Fiddes) was ever allowed to witness a birth in St Kilda it was never certain that the mixture was actually applied. There is no doubt, however, that the Rev Fiddes and hygiene finally won the day. The last death from infant tetanus was recorded on 18 August 1891. But the cost of a high rate of infant mortality to the population of the island over so long a period was not to be recovered.

POPULATION OF ST KILDA 1697–1930

1697—180	1822—108	1906—78
1730—*c.*30	1838—92	1910—77
1758—88	1841—105	1911—80
1764—92	1851—110	1920—73
1795—87	1861—78	1921—73
1799—100	1866—77	1928—37
1803—97	1871—71	1930—36
1810—100	1877—76	1931—0
1815—103	1884—77	

After the smallpox epidemic of 1724 the population of St Kilda had climbed back up to 100 by the end of the 18th century, but it had then levelled off. It never regained the 180–200 mark, which, from Martin's description of life on the island, had probably been the stable and optimum level of population for some length of time. Since there was no contraception, a surplus of food and plenty of room on the island, and as the women married young and disease was rare, in the early history of St Kilda the population problem was more a question of too many people rather than too few— though a high proportion of violent deaths helped to keep control. 'The men seldom grow old,' wrote Sir Robert Moray in 1678, 'and seldom was it ever known that any man died in his bed there, but was either drowned or broke his neck.' By the 19th century the pattern had changed. Fowling accidents had become comparatively rare and death by drowning even rarer. Between 1830 and 1886 only seven people died by accident at the cliff-face and in the same period there was only one albeit serious boating mishap. The most popular euphemism for death in St Kilda nevertheless remained a fowling expression—rather than talk of someone having 'passed away or departed', the islanders referred to their having 'gone over it'.

An imbalance between the sexes in favour of women may always have existed in St Kilda, since the dangerous work of fowling and fishing was mostly done by men, but when disease (particularly infant tetanus) took over as population controller the women established a comfortable lead over the men. They also lived longer. Of the six islanders who died above the age of sixty between 1855 and 1876, five were women (respectively 75, 83, 84, 86, 88) and one was a man (63). Again in 1861 the only islanders over sixty had all been women; below that age the two sexes were almost equal in number. The numerical superiority of women (especially old women) put a strain on the economy of the island, for although they worked hard they were not earners and had to be supported. Perhaps as a consequence of the plentiful supply of women the marriage age went up. In 1877 the average age of married women was $43\frac{1}{2}$, but at the same time the average number of children to a marriage was nine. The high birth rate compensated the high infant mortality.

Tetanus prevented the population of St Kilda from increasing, but no single factor can be taken in isolation as the chief cause of its decline. There can be no doubt, however, that the emigration of forty-two islanders to Australia in 1851 and 1856 had a decisive effect on the fate of the community. Instead of reaching *c.* 115 the population crashed to *c.* 70, where it remained more or less stable until the 1920s, but by then the young men regularly left the island as soon as they were old enough. It was only a question of time before evacuation became inevitable. The decrease in population was both caused by and the cause of a number of determinants, including demoralization and economic failure, which combined to create a vicious circle of decline from which the community was never to emerge.

CHAPTER TEN

Arcady Despoiled

'It was thus apparent that they were excluded from the world, as so many Robinson Crusoes; and though the life of a Robinson Crusoe, or a few Robinson Crusoes, may be very picturesque, humanity will always desire to restore a Robinson Crusoe back to the community of the world.'

ANTHONY TROLLOPE

Among those St Kildans who emigrated to Australia in the 1850s, Ewen 'California' Gillies was the only one who ever came back to live on Hirta and tell of his experiences in the world. Ewen Gillies was born in 1825 and at an early age acquired a taste for adventure restrained only by his native instinct for self-preservation. When he was eight years old he was invited by the factor to try his first cup of tea. Ewen took the tea, but, suspicious of the factor's motives, warned him, 'If I am killed, you will be blamed for it.' But the tea did him no harm and he grew up to be a successful cragsman. At the age of twenty-six, though newly married, he sold up all his sheep and cattle on the mainland for £17 and set sail with his young wife and four other St Kildans in the *Priscilla* bound for Australia.

The voyage lasted more than three months, but twenty days after embarkation an epidemic of measles broke out on board. It was followed on reaching Port Philip by a second epidemic of scarlet fever. Eighty of the immigrants, mostly Highlanders, never even saw 'the land of opportunity'; but the Gillies family survived. On his arrival in Melbourne Ewen took a job splitting wood for a brickmaker called Walstab of Brighton, but after six months he was sacked for laziness and set out across the unmapped territory of Victoria to look for gold. In two years he had made enough money to buy a farm, though not quite enough to make a success of it. After struggling hard for a year or so, dreaming all the while of easier profits to be made in the gold fields, Ewen packed it in. He returned to Melbourne, where he deposited his wife and two children with friends and set out for New Zealand, once more on the

trail of gold. In eighteen months he came back with little to show
for his efforts and to find that his wife had given him up for good
and remarried. Flat broke and upset more by the loss of his children
than his wife's infidelity, Ewen reluctantly left them in the care of
their new father and set off for North America.

There he joined the Union army and fought in the Civil War,
but in 1861 he deserted and escaped westwards in the Great Gold
Rush. In California he finally made his fortune, and when he had
prospected and worked the mines for long enough decided to go
back to Australia to reclaim his children, whom he could now
afford to support. After a brief struggle with his wife he took his
children back and quitting Australia set sail for his native St Kilda.
He spent only five weeks on the island, where he was at once re-
christened 'California', before wanting to leave again. He sailed
for the United States, settled his children there and eleven years
later returned to St Kilda.

This time he stayed long enough to marry another St Kilda girl
before setting out for Melbourne. But California's new bride did
not take to Australia and brought him back to live in St Kilda. Restless as ever California earnestly set about showing the islanders how
to better themselves. He tried to make them change their established
ways and to introduce modern methods of doing things, but after
their initial interest had worn off, the St Kildans tired of California
and soon came to regard him as a very great bore. Finally they were
left with no alternative but to ask him to leave the island and not
come back. In June 1889 Ewen Gillies and his wife sailed the
Atlantic for the last time and settled in Canada, where they lived
a while then died.

California was the first and last St Kildan to try consciously to
improve the lot of his fellow islanders by bringing them up to date
with the modern world, but his enthusiasm for reform was shared by
a large number of outsiders with even less understanding of the
difficulties involved. The end decades of the 19th century were pip-
ing times for professional philanthropists and to some of them St
Kilda appeared as an ideal target for their well-intended but often
indiscriminate arrows of charity. Their eagerness to help expressed
itself in different ways. One Edinburgh man wanted to go and live
with the St Kildans to show them how to get more out of fowling,
though mercifully he was dissuaded from doing so by practical con-
sideration of the hardships involved. In 1859 a West Indian called
Kelsall bequeathed the sum of £600, to be held in trust for the
islanders and only used in times of adversity. The fund, however,

was managed by the Highland and Agricultural Society, who supplied the St Kildans with boats, ropes, corn and other basic necessities with a freedom which was not altogether in keeping with the conditions of Kelsall's bequest.

Gifts and eleemosynary contributions came in all sizes, shapes and wrappers, but perhaps the most significant were those that carried the label marked 'Change'. Crusaders like Connel and Sands, who took trouble and time to get to know St Kilda and its problems, wanted to introduce basic reforms in the islanders' way of life and the organization of their economy. Inevitably the proprietor and his outdated system of managing the island came under fire. In the late 1870s John Sands accused MacLeod in the columns of the *Scotsman* of exploiting the St Kildans by monopolizing their produce instead of allowing them to trade freely with the mainland and other islands. MacLeod replied to the letter : 'If the inhabitants of St Kilda can be enabled to buy and sell for themselves, I shall be very glad to be relieved of a very onerous duty; but the care of the people should not be taken out of the hands of their proper protector, unless there is some security that the change is not one of merely experimental sentimentality.' All too often this was precisely what was behind the suggested reforms. The progressives wanted change for its own sake and saw as the causes of the community's failure many of the traditional aspects of its culture, which to them seemed antiquated and different, but to the St Kildans were important. Brave and keen though they were the crusaders failed to see that their own do-good interference was aggravating and even instigating the very problems which they themselves were setting out in such good faith to solve.

Charity, as well as being the voice of the world, begins at home. In the case of St Kilda, it began at Dunvegan. Far from exploiting the islanders the MacLeod landlords of the late 19th and early 20th centuries were expending considerably more on their tenants than they received in return. Not only did payment of the rent fall more and more into arrears and occasionally have to be waived altogether (in the last fifteen years of its existence the community lived rent free), but the islanders had to be supplied with an increasing variety of goods and services from the mainland which they could not pay for themselves. In 1878 Anthony Trollope, who made a brief call at St Kilda on his way to Iceland, described MacLeod's responsibilities: 'He has it upon his shoulders, and on those of his sister, the onerous task of sustaining by his private means the existence of the community and of relieving their wants. . . . It is good to find a man who will do this, but it is not good to have a state of things in which such doing is necessary.' The proprietor himself, however, had unwillingly helped bring about this state of affairs in the first place.

In 1860 Sir John Macpherson MacLeod had built at his own expense sixteen new cottages on Hirta to replace the improved black houses which the islanders put up themselves in 1834 under the guidance of Neil Mackenzie. The older buildings were not destroyed but kept on as byres and out-houses, while the new cottages were slotted in between them at intervals of fifteen to twenty yards along the street. Of a standard type, probably taken from an architectural pattern book or an illustrated agricultural journal, the cottages were considered at the time to be the most advanced of their kind in all the Hebrides. Each house measured 33 feet by 15 feet and was divided into two or three rooms (sometimes two families shared a house), with a window on either side of the front door looking out over the Bay, and a chimney at either gable-end. The walls were built of stone and cement, harled and white-limed; the roofs were gabled and plated with zinc. At first the cottages had mud floors but in the late nineties they were covered over with cement on the kitchen side and boards in the bedrooms, while the walls were lined with match-boarding.

Soon after the houses had been put up in 1861 a storm carried off most of the roofs. Replacement sets of zinc plates were sent out from the mainland before the St Kildans had time to discover that the zinc roofs were far from satisfactory. Not only did they let the rain in, but they also acted as condensers, so that the houses were almost permanently damp. Luckily a few years later another storm gave a repeat performance—this time the zinc was replaced with felt and tar and the roofs more securely fastened. But there were other ways in which the new cottages were unsuited to St Kilda. Because they faced seawards and had a hard rectangular shape (as opposed to the rounded corners of the old houses) they were particularly vulnerable to easterly and southerly gales. When the wind blew the smoke from the fires could not rise out of the chimneys, and because the door was central between the two chimneys, draughts percolated through both rooms. The wind outside whined like a poltergeist and clamoured at the angles of the walls, which were much too thin for the climate. In short the new houses were damp, cold and draughty, and the St Kildans took time to adapt both to the cottages and to the new life-style which they engendered, some of them preferring to live on in their old homes, others continuing the old way of life in the new.

The most serious drawback of the 1861 cottages was that they had been built by MacLeod's estate masons from Dunvegan and not by the islanders themselves. This meant that they had to be maintained from outside with materials and methods foreign to the island. It was the beginning of dependence on a significant scale. By building the cottages MacLeod had created new needs which could not always be satisfied, and by removing one of the islander's most basic responsibilities to himself and to his family—to put a roof over their heads and keep it there—he had helped demolish his self-reliance.

As the St Kildans became less capable of supporting themselves they grew to rely more on charity, and even began to expect it as their due. In 1879 they sent a message back to the mainland asking for thirty-six tons of coal to be delivered to the island to see them through the winter, but made no comment as to who was to pay the bill. On another occasion they set fire to a brand new boat, which they had just been given, because it was not quite what they wanted; they hoped by their action to be given another more to their liking. And when presented with a gift of rope from James Burns, owner of the Burns Laird Line, who visited the island in 1878, they complained bitterly at the small amount.

When the sea around St Kilda began to be fished regularly and a whaling station was opened in North Harris in the late 19th century, trawlers and whalers would frequently call in at Village Bay on their way to and from the fishing grounds. Before long the islanders were receiving an extraordinary amount of free goods and services from the crews of these boats, whose kindness and generosity were exemplary. The trawlers, mostly from Aberdeen and Fleetwood, carried mail and ran emergency missions for them, without reward or acknowledgement. They made them presents of fish by the basket-load, invited them on board their boats and fed them from their galleys until, at one time, coal and other supplies were being lavished on the islanders so freely that trawler owners had to issue special instructions to their captains to avoid St Kilda waters.

During the First World War St Kilda became a signal station. A naval base was established on the island and for four years the inhabitants, who were not called upon to fight for King and country, enjoyed a kind of false prosperity. They received free and regular food supplies from the Navy and the men were given occasional jobs digging trenches, building huts or as look-outs at 15 shillings a week. But when the station was closed down at the end of the war the islanders were left at a loss, and in the last sad years of the community's existence its dependence on charity was complete. All the needs of the people had to be supplied by the proprietor and various charitable organizations. On education, medical services and religion £500-600 were being spent each year; from 1925 to 1930 the medical bill alone came to £1,642 8s 7d. And the islanders could give little or nothing in return.

Charity never meant much to the St Kildans. As a people for whom the sharing of property was the norm, they were hardly in a position to appreciate its negative influence. The laws of the commonwealth, however relaxed they may have become, could not allow a state of affairs to develop, where one man was in a position to bestow destructive bounty on another—the very interdependence of the people made it impossible. When charity began to flow in from outside the St Kildans had no difficulty in taking what they almost felt was theirs by right, and because they found acceptance so easy, the effects were the more insidious. The St Kildans were proud people, but their pride did not lie in possession and consequently charity in itself could not hurt it.

Sometimes they reacted, not so much to the gifts as to the spirit in which they were given. On one occasion in the summer of 1890 a party of people from Sunderland in Co. Durham decided to visit the island expressly for the purpose of attending the marriage of the Queen of St Kilda, then the twenty-three-year-old Annie Ferguson, to a young cragsman called Neil Gillies. The tradition of the Queen of St Kilda had become very popular with tourists and the expedition was intended half as a curiosity jaunt and half as a sort of do-gooders phantasmagoria. Its organizer, a warm-hearted man (with the best of intentions), called Ian Campbell, had chartered a steamship for the occasion and even put advertisements in the local papers asking tradesmen to donate suitable wedding presents for the bride and groom. Gifts for the young couple, and the other islanders too, poured in. There was a fashionable gown to serve as a wedding dress for the bride, some silver spoons, a wedding cake, a heap of pork pies, jars of Bovril, feeding bottles, bottles of digestive syrup, some old books, a tangle of assorted spectacles and a large American organ.

Before the expedition set off Ian Campbell received a letter from John Ross, the school teacher in St Kilda. Perhaps a little soon in its high-flown praise, the letter read: 'You have done for them, sir, what they cannot sufficiently appreciate, you have led the way, and that well, in bringing St Kilda into true civilization and making it part of Great Britain.' Things did not turn out quite as they had been planned. The wedding party arrived in Village Bay and was met in the usual manner by the St Kildans, who took them for an ordinary boat-load of tourists. But when the islanders discovered the purpose of their visit and set eyes upon their great pile of useless offerings, they reacted strongly and refused to let the people of Sunderland stay for the wedding. The presents were all rejected and, only when the boat had gone, the couple were married without fuss.

Slow to understand the more serious implications of living off charity, the St Kildans were sensitive to the condescending attitude with which it was often handed out. They objected to being treated as wayward and primitive freaks; to being guided on to the path of progress and 'true' civilization by the self-adulating generosity of trippers. 'I do not wonder that they dislike foreigners', wrote Heathcote in 1900, 'so many tourists treat them as if they were wild animals at the zoo. They throw sweets at them, openly mock them, and I have seen them standing at the church door during service, laughing and talking, and staring in as if at an entertainment got up for their amusement.' The islanders' way of life, which had received more attention from writers and journalists than it merited, suffered from this over-exposure, from the scornful curiosity of visitors and the resulting devaluation which their customs and rituals went through in their own eyes. But as the profits of tourism came to buoy up and even dominate the economy of the island their resentment had to be buried.

In 1877 John McCallum advertised for a voyage to the 'Romantic Western Isles and Lone St Kilda' on board a ship of his line, the *Dunara Castle*. She carried forty passengers cabin class, who for £10 could take a ten-day trip in reasonable comfort, if the weather was fine, through some of the finest scenery in Britain. The climax of the voyage was undoubtedly St Kilda, 'the island that wants to be visited', as the brochure put it, not only because of its rare beauty and the excitement of venturing upon the Atlantic, never quite knowing whether it was going to be calm enough to land in Village Bay, but also because of the romantic image of the 'lone isle' and its brave little population. The authors of St Kilda, from Martin to Heathcote made popular reading and many visitors came forearmed. The myth of the Noble Savage still hung over from the 18th century, though for some it had been updated by the theories of Darwin; but the hope of stumbling upon Utopia or at least of enjoying the great moral curiosity of a primitive society in Victorian Britain was never far from the visitor's mind.

St Kilda was always in the news. Anyone who could put pen to paper wrote about their recent visit to the island, and once the novelty of going there had worn off, they wrote about the best way to change the place, to bring it into line with the rest of the country, to save it from itself. Controversy, to the delight of the steamer companies, boosted tourism, and as more light was turned on to St Kilda, the visitors flocked there the merrier. There were two categories of tourist: the trippers, who, like the wealthy yachtsmen, the scientists, the ornithologists, doctors and writers, came for a serious purpose; and the trippers, who simply came for the scenery and a stare at Britain's most backward people. Both in their different ways did equal harm to the inhabitants.

The first steamer ever to visit St Kilda was a ship from Glasgow called the *Vulcan*, which appeared in Village Bay in July 1838 with a full passenger list and a brass band all out on deck. The islanders, who had never seen a steamship before, rushed over to the manse to tell the minister that there was a ship that had caught fire in the Bay. When the band came ashore and marched up to the village to the sound of trumpet and drum with the idea of giving the natives a thrill, they were terrified and cattle, dogs, women, children and men all took to the hills and hid over in Gleann Mor. From 1850 onwards St Kilda was frequently visited by private yachts and government ships, but the tourist trade did not really get under way until the *Dunara Castle* began her regular cruises in the 1870s. She was soon joined by two ships belonging to Martin Orme, the *Lady Ambrosine* and the *Hebridean*, and until 1939 McCallum, Orme and Co provided a regular summer service to St Kilda.

The 'steamer season' became the most exciting and important part of the islanders' year. From the beginning of June until the end of August they did little else except wait for the arrival of the next steamer, while they discussed, both in and out of parliament, taking care not to omit a single detail, the visit of the last one. When a steamer was due they smartened themselves up and put on their best Sunday clothes. The men rowed out to the ship to bring the passengers ashore, charging a shilling a head, while the women came down to the landing place to meet them with baskets of eggs, bunches of marigolds, white heather and other mementos. The tourists rarely spent more than half a day on the island, but their time was well filled. At a price the St Kildan cragsmen could often be persuaded to put on a display of climbing and fowling, which was watched in awe by those who had the stomach for it; others more squeamish preferred to walk over the island and take in some of its more famous points of interest such as the Amazon's house, the Mistress Stone and the Well of Virtue. But from the islanders' point of view the most important part of their visit was the time set aside for trade.

The visitors wanted souvenirs and the St Kildans were happy to oblige them with everything and anything they had. Sheepskins, wool, tweed, scarves, socks, gloves, fulmar wings, gannet's beaks, blown birds' eggs, even old spindles, querns and personal belongings like clothes and brooches were sold without qualms. The islanders' natural talent for barter came into its own, but was perhaps misinterpreted by the tourists, with whom they soon acquired a reputation for being lick-pennies. Money was still a relatively new idea in St Kilda and neither its conventions nor its value were entirely appreciated by the islanders. On one occasion in 1860, when the *Porcupine* was visiting the island, the captain invited some of the inhabitants to look round his ship, but was a little taken aback when they demanded some money of him for their trouble. More understandably they also liked to be paid for having their photographs taken. As is so often the case the first tourists were charmed by the innocence of the people and consequently liberal with money and gifts, leaving those who came after to deal with the dollar-hunger which they had created. With the charm of naivety faded—the islanders soon learnt to lay it on thick especially for their benefit—the tourists became tighter with money, but the St Kildans, who could not understand this change of attitude, continued to press them for pennies as before. Once money had been introduced into their lives its acquisition became a necessity. Influenced by the tourists, their tastes became more sophisticated, their needs multiplied. They lost interest in producing their own food and began to buy in food and goods from outside, becoming more dependent on communications with the mainland. But the tourist industry which had created these needs and given St Kilda its new cash economy was an uncertain source of revenue. The season was short, the public capricious and by the beginning of the 20th century the vogue for St Kilda had died the death.

The islanders gradually became disillusioned and demoralized.

The malign and cumulative influence of tourism, religion and disease; the running down of their economy, the lack of demand for St Kilda produce; the growing dependence on charity and contact with the outside world, combined to give them an oppressive sense of failure and helplessness. The St Kildans ceased to believe in themselves; they relinquished their responsibility to survive and left the matter in the hands of fate. As a people their character, without losing its basic integrity became pronounced in many of its worst aspects. Superstition flourished, parsimony turned to avarice and what had been the easy rhythm of the old life became laziness. A community, which had once been united, were now split by strife and feuds. Very often the troubles had to do with church matters, especially during the reign of the Rev Mackay. George Murray, the student teacher from Aberdeen University, described and commented on some of the cross-currents of discord in his diary. The entry for 23 October 1886, reads:

'This morning I am told that few on the island have seen such a night as there was last night. An old woman of eighty fighting with her daughter, a married woman. It came to blows. . . . After breakfast I went up the hill for a walk. I had not gone far when I saw the people removing furniture from one house to another. A family removed in consequence of the row. No sooner was this finished than another wicked woman began with her evil tongue speaking scandalous things about a married young man whom she declares she had something to do with herself. He flatly denies the charge laid against him. She is and has been a dangerous woman and yet I understand she is a great favourite at the Manse. . . . One cannot help coming to the conclusion that morality is at a low tide in St Kilda. A great change for the worse has come over the island during the last thirty or forty years.'

The climate of dissension was created by small things, such as the special part played by the minister in the life of the community or the inability of the island's system of property sharing to deal with the influx of gifts and manufactured goods. It was still easy enough to divide up the fulmar catch or a basket of eggs, but to turn a Hammond organ or a portrait of Queen Victoria into sixteen equal parts was not really feasible. This kind of anomaly underlies the tragic conflict between the old and the new which gradually destroyed the structure of St Kildan society. Modern civilization soon replaced the island's own culture with a new set of values, which were in no way adaptive to life on Hirta. At the same time the old cultural pattern had depreciated and could not respond to the new conditions of existence. The islanders, caught between loyalties to a disjoined past and an unattached future, became alienated. For a simple society to come through the painful process of adapting to a more complex civilization it must be prepared to renounce its old ways. In the case of St Kilda giving up the old culture meant giving up the island itself.

CHAPTER ELEVEN

Evacuation

'In the Hebrides, the loss of an inhabitant leaves a lasting vacuity, for nobody born in other parts of the world will choose this country for his residence; and an island once depopulated will remain a desert, as long as the present facility of travel gives everyone who is discontented and unsettled the choice of his abode.'

DR JOHNSON

The need for St Kilda to establish better communications with the mainland and other islands of the Hebrides did not arise until the community was already set on a downward course. As the islanders grew less able to support themselves and became habituated to outside assistance, as their health deteriorated and famine threatened, contact with the world came to be essential. In the past the remoteness of the island had been an important factor in the survival of the community, but when communications with the mainland improved enough to destroy its independence, though not sufficiently to bring St Kilda into the swim of things, isolation became the chief obstacle to its continued existence. An adequate link between Hirta and mainland Britain was never established and up until the evacuation the only way the islanders could send a message in times of distress was either by lighting a bonfire on top of Conachair, in the hope that a passing ship might see the smoke and come and investigate, or by St Kilda mailboat.

The idea of the mailboat was given to the islanders in 1877 by John Sands, who himself had been inspired by Lady Grange's albeit unsuccessful attempts to get word to her friends by throwing messages tied to pieces of wood into the sea. While Sands was staying in St Kilda nine men from the crew of an Austrian ship, the *Peti Dubrovacki*, were shipwrecked on the island and for more than five weeks lived off the hospitality of the islanders. By the beginning of February food supplies were running dangerously low. Sands sent a message attached to a life-buoy from the stranded ship, addressed to the Austrian Consul in Glasgow, asking for help. It was picked up nine days later in Birsay, Orkney and relayed via Lloyd's agent at Stromness to Glasgow. Not long afterwards HMS *Jackal* arrived in St Kilda to take off the Austrian sailors and deliver the much needed food supplies.

The islanders later developed Sands' prototype and produced the standard St Kilda mailboat. It consisted of a piece of wood shaped like a toy boat and hollowed out in the middle to hold a small bottle or tin, which contained the letter, instructions for the finder to post it and a penny for the stamp. The bottle was water-proofed with grease and battened down under a little wooden hatch, which bore the inscription 'Please Open' burnt in with a hot wire. A float made of an inflated sheep's bladder with a small red flag tied to its mast was attached to the hull of the mailboat, which was then ready to sail. It was launched when the wind was in the north-west and more often than not—as many as two-thirds of the letters posted in this way reached their destination—it eventually turned up on the west coast of Scotland or sometimes Norway.

The St Kilda mailboats were not before their time. In early September of 1885 a terrible storm swept over the island causing considerable damage to crops and property. On 24 September a mailboat was washed up on a beach near Aird Uig in Lewis. It contained a message written on a sheet of paper torn from a school exercise-book. The letter was from Alexander Ferguson (who later became a tweed merchant in Glasgow) and was addressed to Kenneth Campbell, a trader at Uig, Lewis: 'My dear Sir, I am now going to write you a letter and sending her in one of the little ships in which we were sailing on the shore as you know to let you know all the knews, the men were building a house just a little house for the cows a great storm came on and all the corn and barley were swept away by the storm and one of the boats was swept away by the sea the men of St Kilda is nearly dead with the hunger. They send two boats from St Kilda to go to Haries not the fishing boats but little piece of wood like the little one which I send. I send my best loves unto you,—I am yours truly, Alexander Ferguson.'

The other mailboat had been sent on the same day by the Rev John Mackay and was addressed to Dr Raing, a leader of the Free Church. It had arrived in Lewis a week before Alexander Ferguson's letter and contained certain instructions to Dr Raing to apply to the British Government for food supplies to be sent to St Kilda. In due course the letters took effect and relief came in the form of seed corn, barley, meal and potatoes, delivered by the *Hebridean*.

The St Kilda mailboats inevitably became something of a tourist attraction but they continued to be used in emergencies up until 1930. Attempts were made, however, to set up a more reliable postal service. In 1877 a postal link was established between Fair Isle and the mainland, which immediately raised the possibility of a similar arrangement being made for St Kilda. But unlike the Fair Isle, where steamers from Aberdeen called in on their way to Shetland, St Kilda was not on any shipping route. The GPO could do no more than arrange for the tourist steamers, which visited St Kilda during the summer season, to deliver and collect the mails of the inhabitants. By 1895 there were only six posts to the island in the year and all within the June–August period; for the remaining nine months St Kilda was still cut off from the mainland. Even the island's factor had given up making independent voyages to collect the rent and instead took the option of a comfier and cheaper berth on the *Dunara Castle* or the *Hebridean*. In winter the islanders had to rely on trawlers sometimes putting into Village Bay and out of kindness taking letters and stamp money to post on their return to land. In 1898 the GPO even authorised mail for St Kilda to be sent to Aberdeen for the trawlermen to pick up and deliver, though no suggestion was made that they should receive payment for this service. At the best of times it was always a haphazard arrangement, entirely at the mercy of the weather and dependent on the trawlers wanting to fish in that area.

On 20 September 1899 to the great excitement of the islanders a sub post-office was opened in St Kilda. It was situated on the ground floor of the factor's house and the following year the Rev Angus Fiddes was appointed postmaster at a salary of £5 per annum plus bonuses. After Fiddes left, the job was taken over in 1905 by Neil Ferguson, the first and last islander to be postmaster, who held it until the evacuation. The post office was later moved to a wooden shack with a corrugated iron roof a little way along the Street between cottages numbers 5 and 6. But although the institution of a post office in St Kilda constituted a form of recognition by the GPO of the islanders' needs, it did not solve the problem of how to get letters to and from the island. The situation, which had not really changed, was never to improve. Until 1930 the islanders continued to depend on steamers in the summer and trawlers in the winter for their mails. In the mind of the government the expense of creating a regular service for a dwindling population in a distant place was not justifiable.

Although it was thought not to be a matter of great importance to the St Kildans whether their correspondence arrived sooner or later, it was beginning to be appreciated that it was now essential for them to have some means of communicating with the mainland in time of crisis. In 1912 a trawler brought news from St Kilda that the people were on the point of starving and needed assistance. The national press headlined the story and the *Daily Mirror* gave it special prominence, even going so far as to organize a relief expedition to quieten the public outcry which it had helped to raise. But the islanders were nonetheless grateful. 'Dear Editor,' they wrote, 'a thousand thanks for your great kindness to the lonely St Kildans in their distress for the want of provisions. Your help reached us unexpectedly, and left us more than thankful for it.' The outcome of the incident was that H. Gordon Selfridge, owner of the famous London store, presented the St Kildans with their own wireless transmitter; but before the station had been set up another trawler reached the mainland with the news that the entire community on Hirta had been laid low by an epidemic of influenza. The Admiralty immediately sent a cruiser, HMS *Active*, with two nurses, medical supplies and food to the island. By the time it arrived most of the inhabitants, many of whom had been dangerously ill, were past the worst, but still in a pitiful state. Since they had been too weak to prepare food, none had eaten for several days. The church was converted into a hospital and the schoolhouse into a kitchen and after the islanders had been given food and medical attention, they all recovered.

Work resumed on the Selfridge radio and on 22 July 1913 it was ready to transmit. The resident missionary, Mr MacArthur, was taught how to operate the machine, but unfortunately not how to mend it. It broke down almost immediately and stayed that way until the beginning of the War, when it was made operational again as part of the Navy's signal station. On 18 May 1918 the wireless transmitter was destroyed by a shell from a German submarine. The island was under constant bombardment for nearly an hour and though more than sixty shells were fired there was no loss of life and relatively little damage done to property. But the Selfridge radio had been put permanently out of commission. The St Kildans were neither surprised nor particularly upset since they believed it to have been jinxed from the very start. In a sense they were right, but the wireless was never under any spell, it had simply come too late.

The disastrous events of 1912–13 were not so much evidence of the need for improved communications with the mainland as a final testimony against the viability of the community. Evacuation was again put forward as a possible solution to the islanders' problems. The idea had been in circulation since the mass emigration to Australia in 1856, but it was not discussed seriously until 1875, when a plan was put forward to ship the remaining inhabitants out to Canada. A debate was carried for a while in the columns of the *Scotsman* and the *Glasgow Herald*, but nothing came of it. At that time most of the people wanted to stay in St Kilda. Ten years later they seemed to be all for leaving the island and different ways of helping them to go were examined, but again without result.

Things had nearly come to a head in 1913, but were finally prevented from doing so by the outbreak of war a year later. The comparative prosperity, which the Navy base brought to the island took some of the heat out of the evacuation issue. After the war was over the community struggled on for another ten years, during which time many of the old people died and nearly all the young men left the island for the mainland. The population fell from 73 in 1920 to 37 in 1928, leaving 15 men and 22 women for whom existence had been reduced to a miserable level. Successive crop failures due mostly to bad weather were followed in 1929 by an epidemic of wet eczema which prevented the gathering of the harvest. Once more the St Kildans were threatened with famine. The future had never looked so bleak; but when two ex-St Kildans, descendants of emigrants to Australia in 1856, visited the island and tried to persuade the remaining young people to go back to Australia with them, they refused to leave. Some had only stayed on to look after ageing relatives, but others were still unwilling to give up their world.

It was a small but tragic incident that finally brought home to the islanders the hopelessness of their predicament. In January 1930 a woman called Mary Gillies became seriously ill with appendicitis. Luckily a passing trawler was able to take a message to the mainland requesting medical aid. On 15 February a boat set out from Tarbet bound for St Kilda, carrying mail for the islanders and instructions to bring off the sick woman if her condition was unsatisfactory. But help had come too late and though she reached the mainland and was admitted to a Glasgow hospital, Mary Gillies died soon afterwards. The islanders took her death badly. Everyone knew now that it was only a matter of time before they all left, and as if to make certain they planted no crops in St Kilda that year.

In April T. B. Ramsay, MP for the Western Isles, started making overtures to the Secretary of State for Scotland about the possibility of evacuating the people of St Kilda that summer. The majority were now ready to leave, though some of the older people, who had lived all their days on the island, wanted to finish them there, where their friends and relatives, whom they had no wish to forsake, were buried. On 10 May a petition, signed by all the householders, widows and everyone of working age on the island and witnessed by the missionary, the Rev Dugald Munro, and the nurse, Williamina Barclay, was sent to the Secretary of State. 'We the undersigned the Natives of St Kilda hereby respectfully pray and petition Her (sic) Majesty's Government to assist us all to leave the island this year and to find homes and occupations for us on the mainland. . . . We do not ask to be settled together as a separate community, but in the meantime we would well and truly be very grateful of assistance and transference elsewhere where there would be a better opportunity of securing our livelihood.' If help was not forthcoming many of them had made up their minds to leave of their own accord.

It took time, but at length a decision, the product of endless memoranda, talks, pleas, surveys and calculations emerged from the bureaucratic fundament : the evacuation of St Kilda would take place. The various official bodies involved were nonetheless anxious about different aspects of the operation. The Treasury was worried by the expense and considered the estimated cost of 'no more than £500' rather steep. The Admiralty, responsible for actually carrying out the evacuation, was worried about publicity, and with some justification since the danger of the Press going to town on the human drama and making a public show of the islanders' misfortunes was real enough. All summer long journalists and visitors had thronged the island, anxious to get a last glimpse of a way of life that was about to disappear for ever. MacLeod had even received 400 applications from people who wanted to carry on where the St Kildans were about to leave off.

Argyll County Council were particularly worried because they had heard that twenty-four of the evacuees were to be settled at Lochaline. The County Clerk in a letter to the Department of Health revealed his anxiety that 'during the period of acclimatization . . . certain of the islanders self-supporting at present, might, by reason of their transfer to the mainland become a burden on the County'. As it happened most of the islanders, when asked, had expressed a desire to live in the great cities of Glasgow and Edinburgh. Finally it was decided that the majority were to be given houses and jobs at Ardtornish in Argyll, where they would be guaranteed a minimum of 105 days employment a year working for the Forestry Commission. Trees were not something the islanders knew much about, but that could not be helped, they would learn.

On 27 August 1930 the people were kept busy all day helping to load their sheep and cattle on to the *Dunara Castle*. The sheep were wild and difficult to handle; they had been even more awkward to round up; and although the Government had sent three shepherds from Lewis to give the St Kildans any assistance that was necessary, they never managed to catch them all. Some of the sheep had already been taken off by the *SS Hebrides* in July but the majority sailed for Oban with the last tourists and journalists in the *Dunara Castle* at midday on 28 August. That same day despite vociferous protest from the National Canine Defence League the island dogs, objecting even louder than their would-be protectors, were taken and drowned in the sea. The cats were to be left behind to fend for themselves among the St Kilda mice.

It was a dull but calm day. Since early morning HMS *Harebell*, the ship that was to take the islanders to their new homes, had been lying at anchor in Village Bay. With the sheep and cattle away and the dogs dead, the evacuation of the people could now begin. Last things were packed up, possessions carried down to the pier, and the boxes ferried out to the *Harebell*. Most of the heavy furniture, the bedsteads, chairs, looms and spinning wheels, as well as the boats, agricultural implements and fowling equipment had to be left behind. Nobody quite knew what would be needed in the new homes, but they only took what they believed to be essential. When the work of loading was finished, those with the energy and inclination for unspoken farewells revisited remote parts of the islands. The post office, which had sent off its last mail with the *Dunara Castle* was formally closed, its door locked. That night the St Kildans slept in their houses.

The morning of the evacuation promised a perfect day. The sun rose out of a calm and sparkling sea and warmed the impassive cliffs of Oiseval. The sky was hopelessly blue and the sight of Hirta, green and pleasant as the island of so many careless dreams, made parting all the more difficult. Observing tradition the islanders left an open Bible and a small pile of oats in each house, locked all the doors and at 7 a.m. boarded the *Harebell*. Although exhausted by the strain and hard work of the last few days, they were reported to have stayed cheerful throughout the operation. But as the long antler of Dun fell back on to the horizon and the familiar outline of the island grew faint, the severing of an ancient tie became a reality and the St Kildans gave way to tears.

CHAPTER TWELVE

Culture and Utopianism

'Not in Utopia—subterranean fields—
Or some secreted island, Heaven knows where!
But in the very world, which is the world
Of all of us,—the place where, in the end
We find our happiness, or not at all!'

WORDSWORTH

The story of the islanders after the evacuation is not a happy one. Most went as planned to live in Morvern, Argyll and work for the Forestry Commission, but they lacked the determination to begin life afresh. Some drifted to the cities, where they found it even harder to adapt to the different conditions. Although they kept in touch with each other as best they could the bonds which had once united them were broken, the community for ever dispersed. As for the older people, the shock of the sudden and drastic change often proved too severe and many died soon after arriving on the mainland. Some who were not so old died nonetheless of a similar complaint. Others stayed homesick all their lives and wandered back in the summer months to live in their old homes. They were unable to forget and had no wish to do so. Ten years after the evacuation an islander called Alexander Ferguson wrote in a letter to the Earl of Dumfries: 'I think there is no paradise on earth like it. On Friday last I hired a motor-boat to go to Shillay, and standing on top of that island I saw St Kilda under a white cap of summer haze. I felt like Moses when he viewed the promised land from Pisgah's heights.'

The younger people, many of whom were already familiar with the mainland before leaving the island, suffered less from the pains of adjustment. Reclaimed by the world they soon entered into its amorphous ways. Seven of the men, now no longer exempt from military service, fought in World War II—one of them was even taken prisoner by the Germans. When they came back there was little to distinguish them from other demobbed soldiers. But those islanders who survived the aftermath of the evacuation nevertheless retained their identity as St Kildans. A few of them are still living today and take a keen interest in anything connected with their former home. Some like Neil Gillies, who lives in Glasgow, and Lachlan MacDonald from Ben Nevis talk about the past from long memories with simplicity and ease. It is too long ago now for bitterness and almost for regrets, but the abandoning of St Kilda still has a painful bearing upon their lives. Characteristically they accept what happened as inevitable and discuss it quite cheerfully, for even if their muted sense of loss and deprivation were communicable, it is probably not something they would want to talk about.

As they themselves are the first to agree, the need to evacuate the St Kildans was undisputable. The community could not have survived another winter. Its life might have been extended artificially by outside assistance but only for a few years at the most. The islanders were already living on borrowed time and had been since the turn of the century. But they had become aware to what extent their lives were an anachronism. Visits to the mainland had shown up their misfortunes in a light which made them unacceptable, for once the opportunity of relative prosperity, of a decent living to be earned and of a future assured had been revealed, there could be no putting it out of mind. They saw too that the advantages offered by the world would never come to St Kilda, where life could neither go forwards nor backwards since it had long since come to a stop.

Over the years the fate of St Kilda has been shared by many other islands and outlying communities both in Britain and other parts of the world. Today, despite or even because of developments in communications in the last decades, the existence of remote communities is more precarious than ever, as the centralizing influence of technological society is exerted upon them. The need for a modern country to extend, where it can, the influence and benefits of its civilization to all its peripheral areas is a prerequisite of its credibility. The inevitable casualties, the communities, villages, districts, even towns, which retrogress or fail completely are part of the price to be paid for the honour of marching with progress.

The death of St Kilda, however, was more than an example of how some parts of a country have to be abandoned, when, for one reason or another, they cease to contribute to its economic life. Although nominally a part of Britain, St Kilda was a separate culture, subscribed to by people who in many ways had more in common with a tribe of African bushmen than with the inhabitants of their own capital cities of Edinburgh and London. The decline of the culture and some of the immediate causes of its final collapse have been described, but the more general question of why St Kilda died, and indeed why so many communities, cultures and civilizations fail, when others manage to survive, remains to be speculated upon. Because as yet no generally accepted theory exists to explain the breakdown of civilizations, a normal reaction to the process is to stress its inevitability. It may, of course, be the right reaction. Perhaps interpretations of the fall of the Roman Empire, the demise of Ancient Greece, the disappearance of the Aztecs or the Incas and the extinction of countless primitive cultures will always describe more than they explain, but the question will remain. Without presuming to give answers and at the risk of oversimplifying, it may be possible, in the light of what happened to St Kilda, to define certain aspects of the problem more clearly.

Although all human societies large and small may disintegrate or cease to exist for any number of reasons, if there is a single factor common to the various conditions of their extinction, it is the principle of change. In any society or culture, however unprogressive, change takes place at all times; for culture, in the inclusive sense of the accumulated knowledge, beliefs, art, morals and customs of a people, is a uniquely human attribute, through which man affects his environment in his effort to survive and fulfil his needs. An adaptive mechanism by definition, a culture cannot be static; rather, change is one of its most fundamental properties. The social organization of a culture, therefore, is not a vague and mysterious entity with no particular meaning to it, but the way in which people co-ordinate their behaviour in adapting to the demands of life. It is as necessary to the survival of a society as the structural and physiological characteristics of its individuals. Thus in St Kilda the sharing of the fulmar catch was no less adaptive than the prehensile toes of the fowlers or their love of climbing.

All aspects of its culture may contribute to the ecological adjustment of a society, but basically it adapts to its environment in three ways: by technology, by organization and by ideation. Of these, technology has to be the most directly adaptive since one type of environment will demand very specific implements of survival, such as the cleits on Hirta, while another will require quite different ones, whether they be blowguns, snowshoes or fall-out shelters. The organizational aspect of culture is closely related to its technology in that one of the primary functions of a social system is to attend to the operation of the machines which provide food, shelter and security for its people. In its turn social organization is related to the ideational pattern of a culture, which determines adaptive response. It is typified by the behaviour of nomadic peoples, who after spending a few days in one place tend to get restless and feel ready to move on even if the food supply is abundant. Adapted to a psychology of nomadism through ecological necessity, they are accustomed to responding to their environment in a particular way. Similarly the St Kildans had developed a psychology of isolationism, which, though it enabled them to live for centuries on Hirta in perfect contentment, made it very difficult for them to withstand increased contact with the mainland when it came. A stable society is one in which people want to do what they have to do, and by the same token, a decadent society is one in which people no longer know what they have to do, nor even what they want to do.

When change comes to a society the form it takes is naturally affected and to some extent formed by what was there before, or in other words by the existing cultural pattern, which is a powerful symbolic force in the emotional, psychological and cognitive behaviour of the members of that society. The possibilities of innovation, therefore, are always restricted and modified, which makes the adaptive process slow and tend towards reaction when change is too quick or too great. The problem then is one of trying to understand the ways in which different aspects and rates of change affect different cultures. When a society undergoes widespread cultural change, such as war or revolution can bring, it is thrown into a state of chaos; even slight, localized change, brought by the development of supersonic air travel, for instance, will cause a discrepancy between different parts of a culture; but while some societies can assimilate and survive both types of upheaval, others cannot.

In a simple society, under the normal processes of cultural adaptation, change tends to be very slow and limited in extent. When it comes into contact with a more sophisticated society it cannot avoid being influenced by its superior technology, power and ideas and vainly tries to accommodate sudden and extensive innovations. Consequently its rate of change is speeded up beyond the capacity of its adaptive system with the result that it develops inner strain and sooner or later comes to grief. Even if contact is gradual, as it was in the case of St Kilda, the power of the outside influence is such that it cannot be localized but spreads from an apparently insignificant detail, such as the replacement of a stone implement by an iron one, through the entire social fabric.

With survival as the community's main concern, St Kilda had

developed a social system which was a direct response to the exploitation of a specific environment by specific techniques. As a bird culture the community was a success and its stability bore witness to the accomplishment of its adaptive processes. But the more specialized a culture's form of adaptation the more deeply committed it is to its particular environment and social system and, therefore, the more vulnerable to change. In evolutionary terms St Kilda was out on a limb.

As technology becomes more sophisticated and enables man to have greater control over and make easier adjustments to his environment, and as the historical processes of cultural interaction and reaction change societies, the adaptive process becomes increasingly complex. Innovation now takes place at a rate quite unprecedented in the history of the world; nature appears to play a less important role in the lives of men, to have less effect on societies; and the developed countries of the world to share more and more a single technology-based culture, which creates its own uniform environment. But as man's control of nature shows itself to be largely illusory the technological environment, personified by the belt of urban sprawl cinched around the globe from Tokyo westwards to Los Angeles, appears to be threatened on all sides. Pollution in its various forms not only points up the basic dependency of man on the natural environment, but underlies his terrible insecurity in the environment of his own creation, which, because it is less complex, less varied than the natural system, is more vulnerable—just how vulnerable, we are in the process of finding out. Already there is enough information to take most of the wildness out of the speculation, that if, by a linked combination of ecological catastrophes, from the death of the oceans to the depletion of the world's natural resources, modern industrial society collapses, the ensuing waves of destruction, if they do not carry with them most life on earth, will certainly reduce existence in the developed countries to a much lower level.

Ironically the conscious aims of the technocratic state, whether capitalist or communist, centred on simple, lauded goals such as increasing the gross national product, only add to its instability and hasten its destruction. The same can be said for its less deliberate or less vaunted aims. Whereas a simple society adapts directly to its own territory, the modern state has created structures and institutions, which culturally may have nothing to do with the people affected by them, though ostensibly they exist to serve the needs of different subcultural groups. From the point of view of the state, however, it is important that the needs of the people should not be too varied, and so it becomes the function of its organizations to smooth out the differences between the various groups until their needs are identical. In the general conditions of modern society this is easily achieved since basically people are happy to want the same things whether they live in Orkney or Middlesex, Karlsruhe or Dallas. With a TV set for a hearth in every home it could hardly be otherwise. Deliberate pressure, nonetheless, is brought to bear, especially on the economic front, where needs not only have to be homogenized, but created, cancelled and replaced in an accelerating wheel of advertising, consumption and obsolescence.

Although this syndrome requires increasing specialization, the differences between people and groups of people are eradicated by pervasive national or corporational influences which are extended into all corners of the state and even beyond its frontiers. Alaskan eskimos, sugar cane workers in the Bahamas, miners in the Argentine are all still affected by their own environments, but their livelihoods are often determined by economic institutions operating from several thousand miles away. As they become more dependent in this and other respects on the central culture, direct adaptation to their particular environments decreases and the responsibilty of the state—and hence its instability—are gradually increased.

People and particularly young people, react against mass society, which is at the same time the leaven and the dough of the modern state, in a number of different ways, but whether it takes the form of political rebellion, religious revival, dropping out of society or attempting to inflict some form of idealism upon it, their reaction ultimately comes to bear a close resemblance to what they are reacting against. The youth movement, for instance, made uniform throughout all countries by the communications media of the world, in a very short time became a multi-million dollar concern. Revolutionary politics, undergoing the same treatment, also has possibilities as a money-spinner. It only takes a rock star to appear on television wearing a Ché Guevara beret and the streets of London suddenly become unnegotiable for jay-walking urban guerrillas. At every level ideas are bought and sold just as cheaply. The power of the central culture is too inclusive and too insidious to resist successfully. It assimilates dissidence as easily as it erases subcultural differences and in both cases it reduces individual human responsibility. With the hope of effecting change from within obliterated, the idea of dropping out completely, of being reborn or of remaking the world or a part of it according to some model of perfection, gathers more adherents. As modern society approaches breakdown and chaos, by nature of its being the opposite extreme, utopia begins to look like a realistic alternative.

Utopianism which emphasizes the ideal and the unobtainable serves a useful but restricted purpose in as much as it contributes to the process of criticizing and attempting to improve upon the existing conditions of society. Utopias which are at least intended to be realized, on the other hand, and which are conceived as a leap forwards into the light of a new age, have a stronger appeal and on the whole are of more relevance to the present age. Workable utopianism sells best, in the messianic tradition, to the underprivileged and dissident sections of society or to people whose cultural pattern has been destroyed. Christianity, Marxism and Maoism are utopian ideas which men have attempted to put into practice on a large scale. Although in many respects the results have been disappointing, they have set a precedent for the possibility of realizing utopia and have aroused utopian expectation at every level and in every type of society throughout the world.

Despite endless conflict over how it ought to be achieved, the prescription for an ideal society seems to have changed little since the days of the Greek philosophers. Most people who are prepared to countenance the idea of a practicable utopia would agree that to create harmony among men and in nature should be its aim, and that its conditions should include peace, satisfaction of human wants, a combination of work and leisure, equality or something like it, order and shared authority, and love bringing virtue in its tow. The detail of projected utopias, however, tends to change with time. In determining the wants and needs of men in a perfect society the utopian thinker is necessarily influenced by the scientific knowledge and the technological developments of his time, by the current state of affairs and by his own beliefs and assumptions, whether about the future of space travel or the theory that improved social conditions will render man virtuous in the long run.

Even more than by the example of Marxism, the 20th century has been dominated by the idea that for the first time in the history of the world, man now has it in his power through the development of science and technology to construct utopia on earth, and that without revolution or upheaval the Golden Age will gracefully dawn. The twin bubbles of the technological wonderland and the communist state were successfully pricked long ago by George Orwell and Aldous Huxley, whose well-known fears have and still are being borne out by events. But Orwell and Huxley were finally anti-utopianist, mistrustful of man's idealistic aims, his faith in technology, and fearful of his human nature. They shared a more romantic and possibly more accurate view of man, which celebrates the will, unhappiness, difficulty, danger, excess, heroism and grandeur. They believed, in short, that utopia kills soul.

The situation, however, is being turned around. As the dawn of the technological age becomes a reality and brings with it nothing more utopian than the full impact of its potential for destruction; of its capacity for killing soul and body, leaving two-thirds of the world starving and burdening the rest with a superabundance of choice but no real option; the simpler ideals of an anti-technological bias of William Morris and Ruskin not only begin to have a new validity, but appear to offer the only possible course of action if precisely those human attributes, which Orwell and Huxley were frightened of losing, are to be saved. These ideals are expressed today, all too often in a vague and distorted way, across the spectrum of the protest movement, in nature and ecology cultism, in the interest for Eastern religions and Indian tribes, in the meanderings of the cheque-book gypsies and in the attempts to set up communes. A blueprint for utopia, which is technology-based, the brainchild of prophets like Marshall McLuhan or Buckminster Fuller, will, in the present climate of dissident opinion, find little support, however analytically outrageous or unreadable. Since technology has become identified with destruction, partly because of the less attractive uses to which it is put, partly because of the pollution backlash and partly because technology is thought to be owned by the establishment, it is no longer regarded as the key to the Golden Age. After the normal reaction of the pendulum it is not surprising to find in its place at the other end of the swing, nothing more complicated or original than a longing for Arcady.

It is upon this basic nostalgia, common to most men in all time, to get back to a simple, natural state that utopian theorists from Plato to Marx have based their projections of a civilized ideal society. Any attempt, however, to make of the natural harmony, which existed in precivilized society and still does in primitive societies today, a standard by which the modern world can be judged and condemned must be regarded with suspicion. Equally dangerous is the tendency to misunderstand, oversimplify and sentimentalize the primitive way of life. Unfortunately the excesses of romanticism and the absurd myth of the noble Savage in the 18th and 19th centuries already have their modern equivalents in

the celebration of the Red man, the Gypsy and others, the cultivation of simplicity, innocence and non-think and in the ascendancy
of the *faux naïf*. Inevitably the idealization of simplicity by a
sophisticated element of society must lead it into a false position,
but where the dangers are recognized there is no reason why it
should not learn something from that section of mankind, which
though often pitied and scorned by the rest of civilization is alone
in its ability to live in harmony with nature and itself.

It would be difficult to think of St Kilda as a society in which
all the conditions for an ideal existence were present, but it undoubtedly possessed some of them or it would not have attracted
the numerous claims, which hailed it as the lost Utopia—even if
many of these were made by writers who had never been anywhere
near the place. After the appearance of Martin's *Late Voyage to
St Kilda*, which they used as their source and inspiration, poets of
the 18th and 19th centuries carried the theme with a vengeance.
James Thomson, David Mallet and William Collins among others
more obscure praised the St Kildan way of life for its simplicity
and purity.

> Thus blest in primal innocence they live,
> Sufficed and happy with that frugal fare,
> Which tasteful toil and hourly danger give.

The reek of puritan wistfulness and the sentimental verbiage of
nature worship from afar hardly makes out a convincing case for
utopian bliss. But those who had visited the island and were able
to speak with more authority were nonetheless eloquent in their
praise. Martin himself had written : 'The inhabitants of St Kilda,
are much happier than the generality of mankind, as being the only
people in the world who feel the sweetness of true liberty : what
the condition of the people in the Golden Age is feigned by the
poets to be, that theirs really is, I mean, in innocency and simplicity,
purity, mutual love and cordial friendship, free from solicitous
cares, and anxious covetousness; from envy, deceit and dissimula-
tion; from ambition and pride, and the consequences that attend
them.' Martin liked to stress the moral qualities of the islanders,
which in part he attributed to the influence of the Early Christian
missionaries to St Kilda, but he was not above recording their
faults nor pointing out some of the disadvantages of their situation.

Other writers were sometimes more specific about those utopian
conditions which they believed to be present in St Kilda and not
in other parts of the world. 'If this island is not the Utopia so long

sought, where will it be found?' wrote Macculloch in 1819, 'Where is the land which has neither arms, money, law, physic, politics, nor taxes; that land is St Kilda.' Of the happy islander, he proclaimed : 'His state is his city, and his city is his social circle; he has the liberty of his thoughts, his actions, and his kingdom, and all his world are his equals. His climate is mild and his island is green.'

A winter spent living off salted fulmar and hiding in a stone hut from the bite of the North wind would no doubt have cooled the ardour of some of St Kilda's panegyrists, but among their effusions there is nonetheless an element of truth to be found. Leaving aside the physical aspect of living on Hirta, which had its good points too, the social conditions that prevailed on the island in its heyday certainly fulfil some of the precepts of utopianism. Most obvious are the principles of equality and property sharing, but, although attractive to theorists, they remain somewhat equivocal. The basic harmony of existence in St Kilda depended on the way in which people related to one another at a more personal level.

The important feature of St Kildan society was its size. It is unlikely that the population ever rose above two hundred inhabitants, which meant that everybody on the island knew each other. Impersonal contact between people, accepted as quite normal in modern society, was unknown. Relationships, therefore, were fewer but more permanent and because the range of occupations and social activities was smaller, since most of the islanders were engaged in the business of getting food, the different types of relationship which they could have with each other were equally restricted. On the other hand since each individual played several different roles, as fowler, crofter, fisherman, father, teacher, member of parliament or whatever, relationships tended to be on several different levels and therefore more complex. It was impossible to know only one side of a person and equally impossible to have separate circles of friends, since they were all acquainted or related. The voluntary type of social grouping of civilized society—the tennis club, the Methodist Church, or political party—did not exist in St Kilda. The islanders arranged themselves in groups, but membership was more or less compulsory since the groups were based on birth, age and sex. There could be no withdrawal or change and dependency on a particular grouping was much stronger than in modern society.

Conforming to the wishes and standards of other islanders was a condition of well-being and survival both for the individual and the community. The most powerful check on non-conformity was the disapproval of friends and relations. In so far as it existed, law, like religion, was an integral part of the social system, of the various relationships, between the islanders, and had no separate identity. Values, rules and decrees were transmitted orally by the parliament and envalidated by the past and its myths. Explicit legislation was rare since verbal transmission inevitably resulted in continual adjustments being made, of which the islanders were not necessarily aware. Since laws, skills and the cultural heritage of St Kilda changed little over the years old people were respected as depositories of knowledge, history, wisdom and experience. The old were like books, but frequently consulted, not left to gather dust.

Many people, utopianists among them, would regard life in St Kilda as anything but ideal, not merely because of the hardships and lack of comfort and variety but because of the absence of opportunity for individual originality and creativeness, which, though to some extent dependent on the firm support of a culture, are easily smothered by a cultural pattern which is too strong, too well-adapted. Undeniably there was little room for individuality. One only has to think of those eighteen islanders who went to North Uist and all answered together when one of them was asked a question. But then what could the individual achieve in St Kilda? His wants were as simple as his scope was limited : he performed his duties, expressed himself in words and sometimes poetry and music, loved, lived and died. To become an individual in the modern sense of the word meant leaving the island and finding out how happy he had been when his individuality was less pronounced; for, as Martin observed of the St Kildans: 'There is only wanting to make them the happiest people in this habitable globe, viz., that they themselves do not know how happy they are, and how much above the avarice and slavery of the rest of mankind.'

Like Arcadia or the South Sea Islands, St Kilda can only be taken as a model for the type of utopia which depends on isolation from the rest of the world and where scale is a key factor in bringing problems down to a manageable size. The kibbutzim of Israel, the Soviet collectives and Chinese communes are all parts of larger structures and do not fulfil these basic conditions. An ideal community must have a life of its own, be a law unto itself and stand alone to work or fail. Entry into such a society means renouncing the world and being reborn, whether as a monk or a native of Tahiti. People join communities for any number of reasons but most want either to escape, to prove a theory or find some kind of fulfilment. Invariably they make the same assumption that a certain social system will automatically generate the kind of behaviour which has been observed under it, and almost invariably that assumption has turned out to be wrong.

The present boom of the commune movement, especially in America and Britain, shows no more signs of realizing the utopian ideal than any of man's attempts to create perfection on earth. It is significant, however, that a growing number of people are expressing their dissatisfaction with existence in the modern age, not so much in a vain attempt to find perfection, to seek the unattainable, as in the need to return to a way of life in which nature can be seen and felt to play a more decisive role. Any back-to-the-land movement must be founded upon illusions, but they are soon pricked by the realities of life on the farm. The communes may mostly fail or cheat or achieve merely a dull and miserable existence, but they do at least offer an alternative. Until recently an alternative for cranks and freaks only, but as ecocatastrophe promises and the collapse of modern industrial society threatens with ever louder and clearer warnings, people will begin to look around for a basic option.

When Karl Marx first expressed the idea that modern society was approaching a new system out of which the archaic social type would re-emerge in its highest form, he was telling the end of the utopian dream. But as events move towards a future situation, to which ironically the archaic social type may provide the best and most adaptive response, the utopian dream begins to look less ideal and more realistic. For in the event of technological breakdown, widespread chaos, famine and disease the small community formed out of necessity, rather than through idealism, may well be the basic unit of survival for those who wish to maintain freedom and stay alive. The prospect of a better world will remain as distant as ever, and of Utopia the only vestige will lie in that commonplace happiness of knowing what needs to be done and doing it; but as the history of the world or even of an island at its edge, never ceases to reveal, there is no other.

Bibliography

ANDERSON, Iain F., *Across Hebridean Seas*, London 1937.
ATKINSON, Robert, *Island Going*, London 1949.
BOSWELL, J., *The Journal of a Tour to the Hebrides with Samuel Johnson*, London 1785.
BUCHAN, Rev Alexander, *A description of St Kilda*, Edinburgh 1732.
CARMICHAEL, Alexander, *Carmina Gadelica*, Edinburgh 1923–54.
CHADWICK, Nora, *The Celts*, London 1970.
CHAMBERS, W., 'The Story of Lady Grange', *Chambers Journal*, No. 551, 1874.
COCKBURN, A. M., 'The Geology of St Kilda', *Transactions of the Royal Society of Edinburgh*, Vol. 58, 1936.
CONNELL, Robert, *St Kilda and the St Kildians*, London 1887.
DARLING, F. Fraser and MORTON BOYD, J., *The Highlands and Islands*, London 1964.
FISHER, James, *The Fulmar*, London 1952.
FLEURE, H. J., and DAVIES, M., *A Natural History of Man in Britain*, London 1951.
GIBSON, G., 'The Tragedy of St Kilda', *Caledonian Medical Journal*, April 1926.
GORDON, Seton, *Islands of the West*, London 1933; *Afoot in the Hebrides*, London 1950.
GRANT, I. F., *The MacLeods—History of a Clan*, London 1954.
HEATHCOTE, N., *St Kilda*, London 1900.
HERON, Robert, *General View of the Hebrides*, Edinburgh 1794.
HUXLEY, Julian, 'Birds and Men on St Kilda', *Geographical Magazine*, Vol. 10, 1939.
INNES, Hammond, *Atlantic Fury*, London 1962.
KEARTON, R. and C., *With Nature and a Camera*, London 1902.
LAING, D., 'Lady Grange on the Island of St Kilda', *Proceedings of the Society of Antiquaries of Scotland*, Vol. X, 1875, and Vol. XI, 1876.
MACAULAY, Rev Kenneth, *History of St Kilda*, London 1764.
MACCULLOCH, J., *Description of the Western Islands of Scotland*, London 1824.
MACGREGOR, A. A., *A Last Voyage to St Kilda*, London 1931.
MACGREGOR, D. R., 'St Kilda', *Scottish Studies*, Vol. 4, 1960.

MACKAY, J. A., *St Kilda, its Posts and Communications*, 1963.

MACKENZIE, Rev J. B., *Episode in the life of the Rev Neil Mackenzie at St Kilda from 1829–1843*, 1911; 'Antiquities and Old Customs in St Kilda', *Proceedings of the Society of Antiquaries of Scotland*, Vol. XXXIX, 1904–05.

MACLEOD, Lieut-Col., 'Notice on the Present State of St Kilda', *The Scots Magazine and Edinburgh Literary Miscellany*, December 1814.

MACQUEEN, Malcolm, Autobiography, Bute Collection (National Trust for Scotland).

MARTIN, Martin, *A Late Voyage to St Kilda*, London 1698; *Description of the Western Islands of Scotland*, London 1705.

MITCHELL, A., 'Consanguineous Marriages in St Kilda', *Edinburgh Medical Journal*, April 1865; 'List of Accounts of Visits to St Kilda 1549–1900', *Proceedings of the Society of Antiquaries of Scotland*, Vol. XXXV, 1901.

MORAY, Sir Robert, 'A Description of the Island of Hirta', *Transactions of the Royal Philosophical Society*, 1678.

MORGAN, J. E., 'The Diseases of St Kilda', *British and Foreign Medico-Chirurgical Review*, Vol. XXIX, 1862.

MUIR, T. S., and THOMAS, Capt. F. W. L., 'Notice of a Beehive House in the Island of St Kilda', *Proceedings of the Society of Antiquaries of Scotland*, Vol. III, 1862.

MURRAY, George, *St Kilda Diary*, 1886–7, Bute Collection (N.T.S.).

NICOL, Thomas, *By Mountain, Moor and Loch to the Dream Islands of the West*, Stirling 1931.

ROSS, John, *St Kilda Notes*, 1887–8, Bute Collection (National Trust for Scotland).

SANDS, J., *Out of the World, or Life in St Kilda*, Edinburgh 1878; 'Life in St Kilda', *Chambers Journal*, Vol. LIV, 1886; 'Notes on the Island of St Kilda', *Proceedings of the Society of Antiquaries of Scotland*, Vol. XII, 1876–8.

SETON, George, *St Kilda, Past and Present*, Edinburgh 1878.

SMITH, Angus, *A Visit to St Kilda in the* Nyanza, Glasgow 1879.

STEEL, Tom, *The Life and Death of St Kilda*, Edinburgh 1965.

STEWART, M., 'St Kilda Papers' and 'Bibliography of the Island of St Kilda', Bute Collection (National Trust for Scotland).

TAYLOR, A. B., 'The Norseman in St Kilda', *Saga-Book*, Vol. XVII, 1967-8; 'The Name "St Kilda"', *Scottish Studies*, Vol. 13, 1969.

THOMAS, Capt. F. W. L., 'On Primtive Dwellings and the Hypogea of the Outer Hebrides', *Proceedings of the Society of Antiquaries of Scotland*, Vol. VIII, 1867; 'Letter from St Kilda' by Miss A. Kennedy, with notes by Capt. Thomas, *Proceedings of the Society of Antiquaries of Scotland*, Vol. XII, 1876–8.

THOMPSON, Francis, *St Kilda and other Hebridean Outliers*, Newton Abbot 1970.

TROLLOPE, Anthony, *How the 'Mastiffs' went to Iceland*, London 1878.
WAGER, L. R., *The Extent of Glaciation in the Island of St Kilda*, Oxford 1952.
WIGLESWORTH, J., *St Kilda and its Birds*, Liverpool 1903.
WILLIAMSON, K. and MORTON BOYD, J., *St Kilda Summer*, London 1960.

Index